T0418140

Linguistic Justice

The world contains over 6,000 languages and less than 200 states to accommodate them. This creates the important normative question of how to respond politically to linguistic diversity. What is a just language policy? Are language minorities entitled to language protection? Should language rights be accorded to immigrants? Is the universal rise of English as a lingua franca to be applauded or to be regretted?

The most important and comprehensive thinker within this debate over linguistic justice is Philippe Van Parijs. In his bold and controversial theory of linguistic justice, Van Parijs argues that the rise of English is a good thing, as well as that all language groups are entitled to grab a territory on which only their language receives public recognition.

This collection, bringing together some of the most influential contemporary political philosophers, presents a critical review of Van Parijs's theory and gives a state-of-the-art overview of the prevailing positions on linguistic justice within political philosophy. It will be of interest to students and scholars studying philosophy, politics, linguistics, international relations and law.

This book was published as a special issue of *Critical Review of International Social and Political Philosophy*.

Helder De Schutter is Associate Professor of Social and Political Philosophy at KU Leuven. His work is situated within normative political theory and he specializes in language policy, federalism and territoriality. Papers of his have appeared in a range of books and journals including *The British Journal of Political Science*; *The Journal of Political Philosophy*; *Inquiry*; *Politics, Philosophy & Economics*; and *The Cambridge Handbook of Language Policy* (Cambridge, 2012).

David Robichaud is Assistant Professor in Moral and Political Philosophy at the University of Ottawa and a member of the Groupe de Recherche Interuniversitaire sur la Normativité (GRIN) and the Language Management Interdisciplinary Research Group (LMIRG).

Linguistic Justice

Van Parijs and his critics

Edited by
Helder De Schutter and David Robichaud

Routledge
Taylor & Francis Group

LONDON AND NEW YORK

First published 2016
by Routledge
2 Park Square, Milton Park, Abingdon, Oxon, OX14 4RN, UK

and by Routledge
711 Third Avenue, New York, NY 10017, USA

Routledge is an imprint of the Taylor & Francis Group, an informa business

British Library Cataloguing in Publication Data
A catalogue record for this book is available from the British Library

ISBN13: 978-1-138-89266-8

Typeset in Times New Roman
by diacriTech, Chennai

Publisher's Note
The publisher accepts responsibility for any inconsistencies that may have arisen
during the conversion of this book from journal articles to book chapters, namely
the possible inclusion of journal terminology.

Disclaimer
Every effort has been made to contact copyright holders for their permission to
reprint material in this book. The publishers would be grateful to hear from any
copyright holder who is not here acknowledged and will undertake to rectify any
errors or omissions in future editions of this book.

Contents

CONTENTS

Citation Information

The chapters in this book were originally published in the *Critical Review of International Social and Political Philosophy*, volume 18, issue 2 (April 2015). When citing this material, please use the original page numbering for each article, as follows:

Chapter 1
Van Parijsian linguistic justice – context, analysis and critiques
Helder De Schutter and David Robichaud
Critical Review of International Social and Political Philosophy, volume 18, issue 2 (April 2015) pp. 87–112

Chapter 2
What is language? A response to Philippe Van Parijs
Sue Wright
Critical Review of International Social and Political Philosophy, volume 18, issue 2 (April 2015) pp. 113–130

Chapter 3
The problem with English(es) and linguistic (in)justice. Addressing the limits of liberal egalitarian accounts of language
Stephen May
Critical Review of International Social and Political Philosophy, volume 18, issue 2 (April 2015) pp. 131–148

Chapter 4
Lingua franca *fever: sceptical remarks*
Denise Réaume
Critical Review of International Social and Political Philosophy, volume 18, issue 2 (April 2015) pp. 149–163

CITATION INFORMATION

Chapter 5

Cooperative justice and English as a lingua franca: the tension between optimism and Anglophones free riding
David Robichaud
Critical Review of International Social and Political Philosophy, volume 18, issue 2 (April 2015) pp. 164–177

Chapter 6

Language, dignity, and territory
Anna Stilz
Critical Review of International Social and Political Philosophy, volume 18, issue 2 (April 2015) pp. 178–190

Chapter 7

One-way conversation with Philippe Van Parijs
Jean Laponce
Critical Review of International Social and Political Philosophy, volume 18, issue 2 (April 2015) pp. 191–198

Chapter 8

Can parity of self-esteem serve as the basis of the principle of linguistic territoriality?
Daniel Weinstock
Critical Review of International Social and Political Philosophy, volume 18, issue 2 (April 2015) pp. 199–211

Chapter 9

The political value of languages
Rainer Bauböck
Critical Review of International Social and Political Philosophy, volume 18, issue 2 (April 2015) pp. 212–223

Chapter 10

Lingua franca and linguistic territoriality. Why they both matter to justice and why justice matters for both
Philippe Van Parijs
Critical Review of International Social and Political Philosophy, volume 18, issue 2 (April 2015) pp. 224–240

For any permission-related enquiries please visit
http://www.tandfonline.com/page/help/permissions

Van Parijsian linguistic justice – context, analysis and critiques

Helder De Schutter[a,b] and David Robichaud[a,b]

[a]Institute of Philosophy, Katholieke Universiteit Leuven, Leuven, Belgium; [b]Department of Philosophy, University of Ottawa, Ottawa, Canada

This introduction does three things. We first give an overview of the linguistic justice debate in normative political philosophy. We then situate Philippe Van Parijs's position within it, by zooming in on Van Parijs's two major normative claims: the support of the rise of English as the global lingua franca and the defence of linguistic territoriality. Finally, we clarify how each of the essays that follow this introduction relates to those two claims.

In 2011, Philippe Van Parijs has published *Linguistic Justice for Europe and for the World*. As the first full-fledged normative theory of language policy, it is a landmark publication for linguistic justice theory. This collection of essays contains responses to Van Parijs's book from some of the most well known theorists of linguistic justice today.

The goal of this introductory paper is to indicate what linguistic justice is about, to sketch Van Parijs's theory of linguistic justice and to explain the relationship of the ensuing papers to that theory. As we will explain, Van Parijsian linguistic justice rests on two normative pillars: the argument for English as a global lingua franca (EGLF) and the argument that each language group is entitled to a policy of official monolingualism within its territory. Four of the papers following this paper (by Sue Wright, Stephen May, Denise Réaume and David Robichaud) focus on the first pillar. The remaining four papers (by Anna Stilz, Jean Laponce, Daniel Weinstock and Rainer Bauböck) focus on the second, the argument for linguistic territoriality.

Section 1 introduces the recent linguistic justice field, develops a framework for understanding its internal diversity and gives a brief sketch of the theories that have appeared. Section 2 summarizes Van Parijs's theory within the background offered in Section 1. Section 3 gives an overview of the essays that follow this introduction in this special issue.

1

Section 1

The linguistic justice debate is a development within contemporary political philosophy. It is a recent debate. Only in the past decade have several theorists started to come up with some articulations of what linguistic justice amounts to. In 2003, a collection of essays was published on this matter (Kymlicka and Patten 2003). Van Parijs's *Linguistic Justice for Europe and for the World*, which is the subject of this collection of essays, is the first monograph dedicated to working out a theory of linguistic justice.

Theories of linguistic justice provide an answer to the question: what is the just political management of the presence of different language groups within a political community? This question comprises different sub-questions: Should we go for equality or inequality of recognition between the different languages? Should we go for sub-state territories with monolingual policies, or for states that instantiate statewide multilingualism or for some combination of both? Should linguistic minorities receive special linguistic benefits? Should we endeavour to save moribund languages? Should states have one common language that all speak and understand?

In what follows we first describe the development of this small field of research in political philosophy, before giving a stylized overview of the field by focusing on the most common principles of linguistic justice that have been proposed, and on the normative grounds on which those principles rest.

The linguistic justice debate has two direct antecedents. First, it derives a large part of its driving force from the liberalism-communitarianism debate that animated political philosophy in the 80s. In this debate, communitarians like Michael Sandel and Charles Taylor questioned the individualistic and a cultural atomism of the liberalism of political philosophers like John Rawls or Ronald Dworkin. In contrast to liberal atomism, they set out to develop a more culturally embedded picture of the self, whose identity is not understood as autonomously constructed but rather as largely derived from cultural and linguistic media.

The second and more direct contemporary antecedent is formed by the nationalism and multiculturalism debate. In the beginning of the 90s, important attempts have been made to bridge the gap between liberal thought and communitarian concerns, and to make the liberal premise of individual autonomy compatible with the idea of cultural embeddedness. A crucial figure in this second source of influence for the linguistic justice debate is Will Kymlicka, whose argument is, in a nutshell, that (the liberal ideal of) individual autonomy requires a cultural context of choice (Kymlicka 1995, p. 83). This thesis is also present in some form in the accounts of other liberal nationalists (like Miller 1995, Tamir 1995, Moore 2001, Gans 2003) and liberal multiculturalists (like Raz 1995, Carens 2000). Liberal nationalists and multiculturalists are united in defending the moral and political importance of cultural membership, as well as what they see as the political result of this view, the idea that the just accommodation of cultural difference implies granting cultural minority groups minority (or group-differentiated) rights to state support.

Both ideas are rejected by a wide group of theorists who wish to reject the idea of granting special rights to cultural minorities. Some of these favour the liberal ideal of 'culturally blind' political regimes. The best accommodation of diversity and identity pluralism, they say, is a strong separation between the sphere of politics and the sphere of culture and identity. The state should not publicly uphold or prioritize some conceptions of identity or the good life, say the Catholic view, over others that are thereby subordinated. Therefore, what the state has to do is to detach itself, to remain silent over these issues, by not adopting or publicly endorsing any such position at all (see Barry 2001, Kukathas 2003).

Many of the same patterns and positions of the previous two debates are now re-emerging as linguistic justice views. But the linguistic justice debate has one apparent advantage over other debates over identity: it is easier to show for language than for other types of identity-based difference that it is impossible for the state to take its hands off the field of language altogether. In the debate over religious or even national attachments, it is not always easy to argue against the strict separation between the domain of the political and the domain of non-political attachments. The default position in the religious debate, for example, seems to be that the state should adopt a neutral *hands-off* position. Those who defend special rights for religions then have to come up with complicated arguments for the non-neutrality of states. But this default position is clearly ruled out from the start in the linguistic justice debate. The reason is that states need a way to communicate with citizens: states have constitutions, laws and public schools, and in each case, specific languages must be used for this communication. Kymlicka has argued this most forcefully: 'The state can (and should) replace religious oaths in courts with secular oaths, but it cannot replace the use of English in courts with no language' (1995, p. 111). This impossibility is most clearly the case with respect to language: the language public officials use in their interactions with citizens, the language in which the constitution is written, in which the national anthem is sung at official ceremonies, in which passports are printed, in which courts operate, in which public media function, in which primary education occurs, etc. is inevitably situated and not neutral.

So responding to sub-state linguistic diversity with political disestablishment is impossible. States are inevitably linguistically impregnated and we cannot avoid having language policies. As far as linguistic justice is concerned, concepts like 'benign neglect' or 'laissez-faire' or 'neutrality' are confusing (but see Patten (2003) for an account of linguistic neutrality that is not based on disestablishment). We do not have a choice between freedom and regulation, or between neutrality and engagement. Rather we must choose between different forms of regulation and engagement, between different language policies.

Two principles of regulation are common in the linguistic justice field, and most theorists lean towards one or the other. The first principle is to argue for equal treatment of the language groups from the point of view of the state. If the state houses more than one language group, then the ideal is to recognize all of them on a basis of equality. States like Switzerland, Belgium, South Africa, Canada or Spain aspire to realize such a principle (even if existing realities may often be imperfect approximations of that ideal). On this view, states could for instance grant all speakers alike the right to receive state services in their own language. Instruction might have to be offered in all the official languages in public schools. Street signs might all be rendered in those languages and so on. Different modalities exist for the realization of this principle. For example, we could divide the state into multiple territorial units and mandate one official language per territorial unit. Doing so instantiates a territoriality principle, according to which language rights depend on where one is located within the state (as advocated by Laponce (1987), Van Parijs (2011) and Bauböck in this collection). Or we could officially recognize all the official languages in all the units. This then instantiates a personality principle, according to which language rights track the persons wherever they find themselves in the state (as advocated by Réaume (2003) and Patten (2014, pp. 227–231)).

A second position argues for the idea that we should converge on one shared language. States may house more than one established language group, but the state's recognition should only recognize one of those languages. We may for example choose the language that gives speakers access to the widest set of opportunities (see Barry 2001, Pogge 2003, Stilz 2009), or the language of the majority of the speakers, or the most prestigious language, or the language that is easiest to learn for the other speakers, perhaps because it is linguistically the least far removed from the other languages on average (see Ginsburgh and Weber 2011) and so on.

The particular principle of state recognition that is favoured, as well as the particular language(s) that will be singled out for state support, will depend on an underlying account of the goal of language, of what language is thought to be good for. Linguistic justice theorists usually ground their theories in one or more interests in language, which language recognition can then advance. Within the possible set of interests, there are two broad types, which we can term 'identity' interests and 'non-identity' interests.

A first position holds that policies should seek to accommodate people's identity interests in language. Language policies can seek to recognize the identities associated with a specific language. For example, when language groups such as the *Québécois* are able to claim language rights, or when the EU holds an official multilingual language policy rather than organizing everything only in one language, such recognition is given in order to satisfy people's identity interest in their own language. This position sees people's identity interests in language as important enough for language policy to take them into account and to accord language rights to language groups. In devising language policies, language communities should be treated as communities of identity. Scholars like Taylor (1994), Kymlicka (1995), Patten (2001) and Van Parijs (2011) have expounded this view. When referring to such arguments, we will call them 'identity' arguments in favor of recognition. Two such identity arguments stand out since they have become important within the field.

The most commonly referred to identity argument states that language recognition serves an interest in individual autonomy (or freedom). Autonomy, so the argument goes, requires the disposition of a set of options to choose from. Languages and cultures are option packages: they provide us with the options available to us and with the means to evaluate options. Languages and cultures are therefore 'contexts of choice'. Versions of this argument have been put forward by liberal nationalists and liberal multiculturalists, and in basing a linguistic justice theory on the autonomy argument, scholars directly borrow from those antecedents. The argument has been endorsed by, among others, Taylor (1993, pp. 46–47), Kymlicka (1995, p. 83), Raz (1995) and Gans (2003).

This autonomy idea is based on the view that we perceive the world in the linguistic terms passed on to us by our family and people. As a result, we need access to our language (and our language tradition) to be full human beings, to receive a (first) position. Language groups share similar ways of perceiving the world and of perceiving the value of objects within that world. What Avishai Margalit and Joseph Raz say of 'encompassing groups' (which often share a language) is also true of language groups on the autonomy argument: they share 'implicit knowledge of how to do what, of tacit conventions regarding what is part of this or that enterprise and what is not, what is appropriate and what is not, what is valuable and what is not' (Margalit and Raz 1995, p. 86). As a result, without knowledge of the language spoken in the society in which one lives, or when speaking a language which is too small to sustain a full context of choice, one does not have equal access to a set of choices.

This argument has a substantial philosophical pedigree. The idea on which it relies is that language provides people with the means to fully realize themselves. Why is this so? Because to fully realize themselves, people need a horizon of meaning, and this horizon is always (partly) linguistic. The language we speak in a sense discloses the world to us in a situated way. This idea has been cogently expressed by Gadamer, who has argued that to have a world we need to have a language (1975, p. 411). For Gadamer, and for people in the romantic tradition like Johann Gottlieb Herder and today Charles Taylor alike, language structures the horizon within which our experience of the world unfolds (1975, p. 145). Therefore, 'language is the real mark of our finitude', the limits of our language are the limits of our horizon (1976, p. 64). It is only through expressing a thought in our specific language that we are able to come to an understanding of something expressed in another language. Likewise, Herder has argued that if we lose the disposition to think in the language in which we are brought up, we lose ourselves and also the world (Herder 1877, Vol. XVIII, p. 36).

Why should this language identity interest in autonomy be politically secured? The step from having an interest in my language as the context of my freedom and self-realization to state recognition of this language is predicated on the idea that states must take an interest in providing individuals with the necessary preconditions of realizing themselves as full human beings and of leading a good life. If it is taken for granted that the conditions of individual identity must be politically respected and secured, then we can conclude from the self-realization function of language that the state ought to take the identity and self-realization interest in language seriously.

A second identity interest that can be relied upon by language policy theorists is dignity. Rather than being grounded in a concern about the horizon-structuring role of language that was central to the social theory of Romanticism, the concern about linguistic dignity is older and goes back to the defence of European vernaculars in early modern Renaissance thought. According to this view, using someone's language or affirming its status is a way of promoting that person or that group's dignity. A language is a source of collective and personal self-respect and dignity.

According to the linguistic justice theorists who appeal to the dignity interest, people's self-respect and dignity are often affected by the state of their language and by the esteem their language gets from others. Self-respect and dignity, in turn, are themselves very important goods. They provide us with a basis of self-confidence and a belief in our own worth, which are essential to live a full life.

Many contemporary political philosophers have emphasized the importance of self-respect and dignity to theories of justice. Rawls, for example, has attached great value to the importance of self-respect, which he sees as 'perhaps the most important primary good' (1999, p. 386). He also argues that 'self-respect depends upon and is encouraged by certain public features of basic social institutions', and he argues that this social base of self-respect is among the most essential primary goods (1999, p. 319). Talking about the social bases of self-respect, he says:

> these bases are those aspects of basic institutions normally essential if citizens are to have a lively sense of their own worth as persons and to be able to develop and exercise their moral powers and to advance their aims and ends with self-confidence. (1996, pp. 308–309)

On the linguistic dignity view, one such 'aspect of basic institutions' essential to believing in one's own worth and to having self-confidence is equal recognition of one's language. If there are several language groups in a given state, all of which are recognized but unequally so, then this is felt as a direct assault on the dignity of the lesser-recognized languages. If a language is not equally respected, then the dignity and self-respect of its members are negatively affected. As Van Parijs, who grounds his theory of linguistic justice in the importance of 'equal dignity' or 'parity of esteem', puts it:

> [i]n a situation in which people's collective identities are closely linked to their native language, there arises a major threat to the recognition of an equal status to all as soon as the native language of some is given what is unquestionably a superior function. (Van Parijs 2011, pp. 3–4)

So people's self-respect and dignity are often affected by the esteem their language gets from others or from the state. We might then justify different language policies by appealing to the importance of language recognition for individuals' dignity.

But languages are not only bearers of identity, they can also serve interests not related to identity. For example, sharing a language helps people to understand each other better. Language is then an instrument of communication rather than of identity. So language can also further non-identity-related interests. And theories of linguistic justice can therefore be based on the idea that we should above all promote these non-identity interests. What are these non-identity interests? The three most important non-identity interests that tend to be relied upon in formulating theories of linguistic justice are efficiency, democracy and equality of opportunity, which we discuss in turn.

The ideal of efficiency is to produce what we value using as few resources as possible. Every time we manage to produce the same amount of goods using fewer resources, we get efficiency improvements. There are costs that are intrinsically necessary for the production of certain goods, the production costs, but others can, in theory, be eliminated or reduced. Transaction costs are among those avoidable costs. Language barriers represent obstacles to trade, just like geographical distance imposes costs on exchange of material goods (Barro 1996, pp. 31–32, Grin 2006). By making communication impossible or more costly, language diversity can prevent mutually beneficial deals to be closed. One conclusion can then be to invest in reducing transaction costs. Just like we would invest in ways to reduce transportation costs, we will have to invest in interpreters, translators and other ways to enable communication when confronted by linguistic plurality. Note that those extra costs do not improve the communication and the potential transactions; they only make it possible. A language shared by all actors involved in the production and exchange of goods represents a major improvement in efficiency due to the transaction costs that are reduced or eliminated. So it is also possible to conclude that the best way to reduce the costs of linguistic diversity is to eliminate the diversity and ask all to converge on one shared language. For example, Huntington, reacting against the rise of Spanish in the United States, has declared that '[w]ithout a common language, communication becomes difficult if not impossible' (2004, p. 159).

The second important non-identity interest is democracy. Language plays a role in the realization of the political value of democracy. For example, citizens need to understand the language in which the laws are written and stated publicly, and the ideal of a deliberative democracy is easier to realize when citizens speak the same language. Some theorists of linguistic justice have therefore argued that a central pillar of a successful theory of linguistic justice is the extent to which it realizes the democratic interest in language. For example, Daniel Weinstock, who combines the democracy argument with the efficiency argument, has argued that 'the most attractive language policy is one that goes no further in its imposition of the language of the majority than what is required in order for the state to be able to communicate effectively with its citizens' (Weinstock 2003, p. 267).

> In most cases, it will advantage the language of the majority. But it will do so for pragmatic reasons to do with the organization of a functioning democracy, rather than because the majority linguistic community in question is seen as bearing "intrinsic" value, or (...) because the defense of the language of the majority is uniquely just (...) (Weinstock 2003, p. 269)

Likewise, Barry has said that

> [p]olitical communities are bound to be linguistic communities, because politics is (in some sense) linguistically constructed. We can negotiate across language barriers but we cannot deliberate together about the way in which our common life is to be conducted unless we share a language. (Barry 2001, p. 227)

Therefore, 'democratic states that still have an open future [with regard to the possible development of distinct linguistic communities] have every reason for pursuing the course that leads to a linguistically homogeneous polity' (p. 228).

The third non-identity interest is equality of opportunity. Thomas Pogge has spoken out against the possible dangers that come along with introducing bilingual English/Spanish forms of education in the US. Pogge's worry is that the Hispanic claim for the recognition and introduction of Spanish into the public educational system might be motivated more by a concern about the interests of the Hispanics as a group rather than about the interests of the children themselves. He argues that the equality of opportunity interest of Hispanic children overrides the group interest in getting official recognition of Spanish on American soil. As a result, he calls for an *English-First* principle, which he defines as:

> the most important linguistic competence for children now growing up in the US is the ability to communicate in English; and the language of instruction in public schools in the US should therefore be chosen by reference to the goal of effectively helping pupils develop fluency in English. (Pogge 2003, pp. 118–119)

This egalitarian reason for engaging in language politics and for possibly rejecting claims for language rights by linguistic minorities is also one of the basic arguments of Barry, who emphatically endorses equality of opportunity as an argument against the multiculturalist case (2001, pp. 103–109). While he, for instance, does not rule out the possibility of ensuring that Welsh is 'available to be taught in the schools', he does warn against excessive attention to Welsh (and especially against compulsory education in Welsh), since it would come at the expense of the equality of opportunity of Welsh children (2001, pp. 105–106).

So we have a series of identity-based interests in language that can be served by language policy, with autonomy and dignity as the most important ones. And we have several non-identity interests, with efficiency, democracy and equality of opportunity as the most important ones.

There is an important relationship between these interests on which language policies can be grounded, and the principles of recognition that are selected. For example, if one believes that autonomy is all that matters, then that policy will be favoured that makes sure to distribute the language recognition in such a way that each group has a secure linguistic context. If instead one believes that all that matters is being able to communicate with an as wide as possible group of people globally, thereby endorsing the non-identity argument in communication, then we should also converge on one shared global language, either as a shared native language or as a shared lingua franca. That language could in principle be any language, but it might make sense to choose Chinese (Mandarin), which still outrivals Hindi and English, in terms of number of both native and non-native speakers. Or one might opt for Esperanto, which can be defended for its ease of acquisition. Or it could be English, which Van Parijs argues we should adopt a global lingua franca.

In fact, if a language group shares a state or territory with a larger language group, then all else being equal, on the non-identity view, we should try to induce the speakers of the smaller language to get to know the larger language. Doing so will benefit non-identity-related functions of language such as efficiency, communication, equality of opportunity, stability. Of course, it depends on the selected non-identity reasons: it might be that one selects 'linguistic diversity' as a non-identity interest and then the goal can be to recognize multiple languages. But in general that is not what happens: the non-identity interests that are selected are usually majority language or single language favouring interests. The identity view, in contrast, will generally strive to grant similar official status, rights and recognition to both language groups.

Nothing prevents, however, compromise positions between the identity and the non-identity-related functions of language. This is what makes theorists like Patten call the ensuing theory 'hybrid' (Patten 2003, p. 386). We shall see in part two of this introduction that Van Parijs is such a hybrid theorist.

Yet, a number of scholars in the linguistic justice field have taken the view that language policies should *only* seek to satisfy non-identity interests. People may have an identity interest in language, but, this view stipulates, we should abstain from using public policy measures to accommodate it (especially in cases where it would conflict with the non-identity interests in language). Instead we should regulate language(s) in such a way that the non-identity-related goals are realized. This is what drives the views of, among others, Barry (2001), Pogge (2003) and Weinstock (2003).

Other positions are imaginable: in principle, one might take the view that non-identity reasons do not matter and that we should only care about identity interests. One might also take the view that both non-identity and identity interests matter, but that, in cases of conflict, we should prioritize one of both interests. It is also possible to distinguish the non-identity interests more precisely and then design a priority principle that assigns greater importance to some non-identity interests above others. The same can be done with regard to the identity interests.

No matter what the particular mix of identity and non-identity arguments, however, it is clear that practically all arguments for or against language recognition advanced in this debate situate themselves somewhere on the identity/non-identity axis. All arguments appeal, that is, to the importance of language for individuals and states, whether that importance servers identity or other interests. Language is supposed to be good or important for something else; it is not defended as a good in itself. So the distinction between non-identity and identity approaches to language policy is not equivalent to the distinction between instrumental approaches, which take language to be valuable for something else (whether dignity, equality or some other good), and intrinsic approaches. The intrinsic approach, defended for example by Rockefeller (1994, p. 94) and Musschenga (1998) claims that cultures (or languages) are morally valuable in themselves, independent of the value their members attach to them. This intrinsic argument stands opposed to instrumental accounts, which consider only the individual to be the bearer of rights.

The vast majority of existing political philosophies of linguistic justice, however, do not rest on the idea of intrinsic value, including Van Parijs's theory. Most theorists take only individuals to be the bearers of rights. The upshot of this is that languages and cultures matter only insofar as they are desired by individuals. In fact, both the non-identity and the identity views we just discussed present distinctive accounts of what it means *for individuals* to have a language, and thereby already assume that languages are there for the benefit of their speakers.

Section 2

In *Linguistic Justice for Europe and for the World*, Philippe van Parijs builds his theory on two main pillars. The first is a justification of the promotion of English as the emerging global lingua franca. The second is a justification of the territoriality principle, as a means of realizing equal respect for all speakers. Three principles of linguistic justice – cooperative justice as equal ratio of costs and benefits, distributive justice as equality of opportunity and equal respect as parity of esteem – provide the justifications for these two pillars, and offer normative grounds to settle specific disputes regarding the legitimate limits within which these two objectives can be pursued. These three principles generate a compromise between the promotion of non-identity-based interests through the creation of a lingua franca and the promotion of the identity-based interest in esteem through the territorial protection of minority languages at the local level. Indeed both the identity and the non-identity functions of language are for Van Parijs normatively important, and it is the fact that he works out a compromise between them in the defence of the lingua franca and of territoriality that justifies calling Van Parijs a 'hybrid' theorist of linguistic justice.

The universality of linguistic disputes, and the need to come up with a normative discourse to take principled positions in the settlement of these disputes, prompted the writing of a book that is made more necessary as we move forward due to three global phenomena. First, democratization is happening in multilingual countries facing the challenge of bringing together many *demoi*; second, globalization makes interaction and communication across linguistic borders more likely and more necessary than ever before; third, international migration increases the level of linguistic diversity in most countries and regions of the world. What a just world needs is, in a nutshell and as mentioned, a global lingua franca and a territory offered to each language community able and willing to bear the costs associated with it. Now let's discuss the normative grounds for these two controversial propositions in turn.

The most controversial argument is presented in the first chapter of the book: not only should we celebrate the 'natural' emergence of EGLF, we should also accelerate and promote its spread. Van Parijs, offering more than classic pragmatic and efficiency reasons, morally justifies the promotion of a global lingua franca based on two non-identity reasons. First, sharing a global language may create a justificatory community that will trigger an ethical contagion, a viral awareness of the morally unacceptable conditions some individuals live in. This will happen following a multiplication of encounters in which, in one way or another, citizens of wealthy states will be asked to provide justification for their favorable relative condition. Second, sharing a lingua franca will make it politically feasible to act upon this awareness of immoral global inequalities. A global lingua franca will provide the means to deliberate and mobilize across borders, will contribute to the creation of a global demos.

> This common demos, in turn, is a precondition for the effective pursuit of justice, and this fact provides the second fundamental reason why people committed to egalitarian global justice should not only welcome the spread of English as a lingua franca but should see it as their duty to contribute to this spread in Europe and throughout the world. (Van Parijs 2011, p. 31)

Why only English? For efficiency reasons: a single lingua franca is more efficient than many, reducing the costs of learning while maximizing potential communication. Another reason is that EGLF is already in the making. English is the language spoken by the largest number of speakers, and it is the language being learned by the most people. Van Parijs identifies two micro-mechanisms – *probability driven language learning* and *maximin language use* – that not only offer an elegant explanation of the rise of English globally, they also offer reasons to expect and predict that the process will lead to the first truly global lingua franca in human history.

First, the probability of learning a language and the level of proficiency people will reach is related to the probability of speaking the language. We can explain this fact by individual motivation: a more useful language will motivate more people to learn it. We can also explain it by opportunities, since having more opportunities to use a language is also more opportunities to practice and acquire language skills. More people speaking English then means more motivation to learn it and more occasions to practice and improve our language skills.

Second, the maximin language use micro-mechanism describes a tendency we have in multilingual groups to use the language that will exclude as few people as possible. We tend to have discussions in the language known best by the conversation participant who knows it least well. When a Mandarin speaker, a Hungarian speaker and an English speaker meet, the level of English of the Mandarin and the Hungarian speakers (who know it less well than the English speaker) is very likely to be higher than the level of any other language that might be shared in some measure between them. The maximin mechanism is indeed bound to favor English in many conversations involving multilingual speakers and that is true whether or not English native speakers participate in the conversation. For example, English is also likely to be the maximin language if the English native speaker is replaced by, say, a speaker of Arabic.

These two mechanisms then combine and compound their effects, multiplying the situations in which English is used between multilingual speakers and then offering more motivation and more opportunities to learn English. A dynamic process is under way and whether we like it or not, English is becoming a global lingua franca. Van Parijs wants this process to unfold as rapid as possible, but the main normative reason to *accelerate* the dissemination of English as quickly as possible will be presented in the section on distributive justice.

So Van Parijs believes that, for global justice reasons, English should be promoted as the world's sole lingua franca. However, Van Parijs understands that that cannot be the full story. More specifically, no matter how just it is, the process of creation and the maintenance of the global lingua franca may also bring with it a number of injustices. Van Parijs identifies three potential sources of injustices – unfair distribution of costs and benefits, unequal opportunities and disparity of esteem – related to three dimensions of language –

language as collective goods, as productive skills and as sources of esteem. We will discuss these three injustices and their underlying linguistic dimensions in turn.

Firstly, if we see languages as collective goods, the distribution of the costs and benefits of the creation of the lingua franca seems unfair. The cooperative venture necessary to produce a lingua franca enabling global communication will require from non-anglophones to invest important resources (10,000 h on approximation). Learning English will of course provide benefits to learners, but it will also provide substantial benefits to native Anglophones. When someone learns a new language, it offers this person a vast number of new speech partners, but it also provides the latter with a new potential speaker. The problem is that all the costs of the creation of this collective good are borne by non-anglophones who have to invest in learning English. If every English speaker benefits from the learning of non-anglophones and if only the latter are bearing the costs of the creation of this communication good, the situation is unfair.

Van Parijs proposes to equalize the cost-benefits ratio, asking people to bear costs proportional to the benefits they receive from the creation of the *lingua franca*. Details aside, it would amount to a considerable contribution from Anglophone nations to others learning English. Since there are no chances of persuading English-speaking nations to accept a tax aimed at subsidizing English learning around the globe, and since such a tax cannot be imposed by force, Van Parijs proposes an interesting alternative: retaliatory free riding. If English countries free ride on the creation of a *lingua franca*, on the creation of a common good from which they benefit, others should feel free and morally legitimate to free ride in other domains. How? Van Parijs says: Poach the web! Take whatever available from the web and enjoy it without any consideration for intellectual property rights. Poaching the web could suffice to balance the distribution of costs and benefits in the spread of EGLF within fair proportions for every linguistic community.

The second source of injustice is inequality of opportunity, grounded in the fact that languages are productive skills. From a distributive justice perspective, the creation of a lingua franca will create deep inequalities of opportunities first between native speakers and 'new speakers' of English, and second between all English speakers and those unfortunate who would not master it. There are unequal opportunities *to* language, but also, and more importantly, unequal opportunities *through* language. Individuals would not have the same opportunities to speak the language of their choice, but they also would not have the same opportunities offered by the language they are most comfortable in.

Van Parijs identifies four forms of such unequal opportunities: language-related jobs, linguistic requirements for other jobs, media-amplified audience and face-to-face interactions. First, native speakers will be highly demanded around the globe to fill language-related jobs requiring a native knowledge of

English. An increase in demand for English will amount to an expansion of job opportunities for English native speakers, especially in a globalizing labor market. Second, English will become an asset in many types of jobs not language related. All these jobs will be offered primordially to individuals with a high proficiency in English, favoring once again native Anglophones. Third, more English speakers will mean a wider reach for Anglophone media and more people having access to products made available through these media. Anyone offering services or goods available through Anglophone media, either singing, writing, acting, offering formations or conferences will necessarily benefit from more 'customers'. Finally, leaving the increase in working and lucrative opportunities aside, we must also mention that every time English will be used as lingua franca among speakers of different languages, those with native skills will be advantaged. They will be more interesting, clearer, funnier, more comfortable than their counterparts having English as a second language and will tend to reap benefits from this competitive advantage.

After assessing different alternatives, including modification of language regimes, transfers on the basis of unequal linguistic capital or unequal capital taken generally, Van Parijs concludes that the best way to deal with these inequalities in opportunities is by 'accelerating the dissemination of the lingua franca beyond the elite of each country' (Van Parijs 2011, p. 116). Those competitive advantages enjoyed by native speakers of English will tend to diminish as the whole world population becomes more fluent in English. In addition to classic ways of transmitting specific skills like inclusion of English to school curricula, Van Parijs proposes a way to disseminate English that is as surprising as it is cheap: Ban dubbing! Presenting data showing a higher proficiency in English in countries in which foreign movies are subtitled but not dubbed, he argues in favor of a ban on dubbing. Cultural products offered in English will contribute to increase contacts with English globally, at very low costs making it, unlike education, an affordable solution for every nation around the globe.

The third source of injustice is of an identitarian form, grounded in the link between language and esteem. Both inequalities of opportunities and unequal distribution of costs and benefits can be reduced by accelerating the spread of English. They are transitory problems that would disappear as more people learn English. A third source of concern seems, however, to become more acute with such a rapid spread of EGLF: a disparity of esteem felt by speakers of other languages. If we view languages as identity markers, accelerating the spread of English and granting it a lingua franca status would create injustices in terms of unequal respect and recognition of languages and language communities. By granting a special, global and superior status to English, speakers of other languages might feel depreciated linguistically, might feel threatened by this supercentral language, and might resent the fact of having to bow to Anglophones by speaking their language in a more or less clumsy way in a growing number of social contexts. The emergence of asymmetric linguistic practices, in which the same language is systematically chosen in multilingual contexts, could be used as a prima facie indication of the presence of such injustices. This sensitive issue is taken seriously by Van Parijs who devotes two chapters, including the longest one of the book, to the just way to deal with this injustice as disparity of esteem suffered by 'minority' speakers. It is with this argument that Van Parijs invokes an identity interest in language as a basis for language policy: this argument will ground the second language policy pillar of the book: the defence of linguistic territoriality.

A common way to deal with linguistic diversity at institutional level in multilingual states has been to grant every national language, or a subset of languages, the same public status and offer them equal recognition. Each language is affirmed as having official or equal status, can be used in institutions, and is present in official publications and in important communication between the State and the people. Unfortunately, such a solution is becoming impractical and too expensive for political entities like the EU, and things get more complicated each time we add new official languages. The reason why we need a better way to express equal respect for every language community is not the costs, but rather the lack of a legitimate rationale to justify bearing those costs. The pragmatic rationale behind such policies, namely that each citizen needs to understand the decisions made by the institutions and must be able to express their opinions and be understood by the institutions, is becoming weaker as EGLF spreads. If the use of every official language is not necessary for the institutions to work efficiently internally, and for the population to have easy access to the institutions, we are left with a symbolic recognition of each language community as the sole justification for the heavy sums invested in translation of documents and website and the multidirectional interpretation of debates. The rationale seems too weak to support such costly symbolic recognitions. Language communities should recognize that these resources could be put to better use, and if they do not, they should be free to demand that their vernacular language be used on a par with English as working language inside the institutions, as long as they are ready to bear the costs of this expensive preference.

We need a way to express equal recognition and equal respect for language communities sharing institutions. We need something more than mere symbolic recognition, and we need solutions more practical than granting equal status to all languages or to a sample of them, or making the learning of many or all official languages mandatory. Granting symbolic minority rights to every linguistic community is the wrong way to go. The solution proposed by Van Parijs to ensure linguistic justice as parity of esteem is rather: Make every tongue a Queen!

The proposition is to grant a right to every language community to impose its language in public education and in public communication applying territorial separation and ensuring that each language is dominant on a given territory. There are two important aspects to this proposition. First, the regime must be coercive; second, it must apply to a territory and not to categories of speakers.

Presenting a *territorial* application of a coercive linguistic regime, Van Parijs shows how it is superior to a non-territorial or categorical regime by guaranteeing that the bowing will be reciprocal between language communities and would not be unilateral. Ascribing linguistic rights to individuals on the basis of their 'linguistic category' does not ensure that speakers of dominant languages bow to dominated languages in some contexts. Parity of esteem is then better served by a territorial regime than by a personal or categorical regime. Every individual settling on the territory is expected to gain profi-ciency in the vernacular language, to bow to the vernacular speakers in some contexts. Of course, the state will have to guarantee an easy access to resources in order to facilitate linguistic integration, and some temporary linguistic facilities might be necessary during the transition to the coercive regime. Those measures are made necessary in order to respect equal opportunities for all.

Van Parijs then argues that a coercive regime is superior to an accommoda-tion regime where the state practices a politics of indifference towards the maintenance of language diversity and simply tries to accommodate citizens' linguistic preferences as long as these impose reasonable costs. The coercive aspect of the proposition is necessary to counter the 'kindness-driven agony' of weaker languages. A strong mechanism threatening weaker languages is the fact that people are nice to each other. They will not refuse an interaction on the basis that it would be happening in 'the wrong language'. If they master the language they are addressed in, even if this language is dominant and a threat to their vernacular language, and even if they have 'the right' to an interaction in their vernacular language, they will act nicely and switch to their second language. These noble dispositions add to linguistic agony of domi-nated languages by reducing the necessity to speak the local language for peo-ple settling on the territory and by making it likely that, in time, a more dominant immigrant language takes over territory previously predominantly inhabited by speakers of a smaller, local language. Reducing the opportunities to speak the vernacular language amounts to a reduction in the motivation to learn it and to fewer opportunities to practice it, and therefore to more pressure on dominated languages.

The territorial coercive regime contributes to make proficiency in the local language necessary for every individual settling on the territory, and it is made just by the reciprocal expectations it creates: just as anyone settling on the territory of our language community is expected to learn the vernacular lan-guage, we are expected to learn the local vernacular language if we choose to settle in a different language community. If every language community can enjoy a territory on which they are sovereign, we can expect parity of esteem to be attained. A democratic process should determine what communities are to be organized under a territorial coercive regime, local populations being free to decide if the benefits of parity of esteem offset the costs of linguistic integration of allophones and the expectable decreased prosperity due to a net loss in human capital. The borders of these democratic consultations should be drawn in a way that favors small linguistic communities. What parity of esteem requires a right for each language community to implement a territorial linguistic regime to protect itself if the community so desires.

So far we have discussed Van Parijs's invocation of two normative language policy pillars – English as the lingua franca, and linguistic territoriality – and the justifications he gives for them: non-identity justifications of global justice, fair cooperation and distributive justice for the lingua franca argument, the parity of esteem justification for linguistic territoriality. Van Parijs ends the book with one other concern that is often discussed in linguistic justice theory: the value of linguistic diversity. Would the creation of a lingua franca and the territorial regime protect enough or too much of the linguistic diversity as we know it?

Van Parijs claims that there is no guarantee that linguistic diversity, as we know it, will be protected. First, not every language spoken will meet the conditions to become a queen on a territory, and second of all not every language community will be willing to bear the costs that comes with the implementation of a territorial regime. We can even expect a reduction of some form of diversity following the spread of lingua franca and the implementation of a territorial linguistic regime.

First, the territorial linguistic regime will impose some pressure on local linguistic diversity. Diversity can be approached at the local level or at the inter-local level. Local diversity refers to the heterogeneity in a given area, whereas inter-local diversity refers to the distinctive composition of different areas. These two levels of diversity are bound to be in tension. Maximum local diversity is obtained when, for example, each language is spoken in every area; maximum inter-local diversity is obtained when the language spoken in an area cannot be found in any other, that is, when each area is unique. If the number of languages spoken in every area increases, this will contribute to local diversity but will reduce inter-local diversity.

Parity of esteem will justify territorial linguistic regimes that will promote inter-local diversity at the expense of some local diversity. It will increase the number of contexts in which the official language will have to be known and spoken. Even provided that multicultural rights guarantee the freedom to speak minority languages and some forms of linguistic accommodations compatible with the dominance of the local language, we can expect a reduction in the opportunities to speak other languages than the official language.

We can also expect a reduction of diversity following the creation of a global lingua franca. In a world where speakers often have competence in many languages, we cannot ascribe speakers to only one language community when quantifying diversity. One way to approach diversity is then to look at the non-coincidence of language repertoires. The spreading of a global lingua franca will definitely have an impact on diversity so understood since a common language will then be part of a vast number of speaker's language repertoire.

Is this loss of diversity morally problematic? Van Parijs does not think so. Linguistic diversity is, we must face it, a formidable obstacle to mutual understanding. More diversity means less speech partners and more difficulty to access information. We might think that we dispose of strong arguments in favor of linguistic diversity to offset this problem, but according to Van Parijs we do not. Many arguments have been put forward to argue in favor of the value of languages or linguistic diversity, ranging from languages being sources of knowledge for linguists and a source of revenue for translators, interpreters and many others; over the idea that their lexicon, syntax, morphology tell us about the history of the people who spoke them; to the ideas they are repositories of local and ancestral knowledge, offer a unique world view, contribute to cultural diversity and maintain diverse options and opportunities available for individuals.

None of these arguments are very promising if we want to justify the protection or the maximization of linguistic diversity. The last one is worthy of some consideration, since it appeals to the contribution of linguistic diversity to the enrichment of individuals' options in leading their lives. However, if linguistic diversity helps protect some cultural specificity, it also makes these different options inaccessible to those who do not master the language. We can then conclude with Van Parijs 'that no more and no less linguistic diversity is justified than what would be preserved by the territorial regime required on grounds of parity of esteem' (Van Parijs 2011, p. 193).

The final question of the book is of fundamental importance for the prospects of global distributive justice: would such a level of linguistic diversity represent an obstacle to global justice? A number of studies highlighted a negative correlation between linguistic diversity and different variables related to solidarity. Some explanations have been proposed. Linguistic diversity would create a difficulty of identification between segments of the society, namely the worst offs when they are members of a different linguistic community; it might also make communication less efficient, an obstacle to mobilization and to the diffusion of justice claims across linguistic frontiers.

The territorial regime will contribute to redistributive policies and solidarity on a local level, offering to every member of society a common language serving both as an equalizer of economic opportunities and as a part of a common identity and as a mean to the creation of a demos. Unfortunately, such a regime creates obstacles to solidarity at the inter-local level. Adding to the problems of communication and identification the fact that administrative borders tend to coincide with linguistic borders, and we are faced with three potential sources of difficulty for global institutions of justice. This clash between the results of parity of esteem and the pursuit of global distributive justice is 'unavoidable. (Van Parijs 2011, p. 203). We can still hope, with Van

Parijs, that the pacification of cultural and linguistic tension through the implementation of the territorial regime, and the creation of a global demos with the emergence of a lingua franca, will both contribute to a stable and satisfactory trade-off between linguistic justice as parity of esteem and global economic equality as real freedom for all.

Note that, with this argument, Van Parijs rejects the case for linguistic diversity on two grounds we discussed before: he rejects the idea that linguistic diversity has intrinsic value; and he rejects the idea that it should be pursued for non-identity-based purposes. Diversity has no intrinsic value since for Van Parijs language only ought to be protected or recognized when their speakers demand such protection; language has no value in and of itself apart from the value it has for its speakers. And he rejects the idea that linguistic diversity is desirable for non-identity reasons: only when speakers claim language recognition for dignity reasons is a particular language worthy of (territorial) protection.

Section 3

Above we have shown how Van Parijs's normative proposals rest on two major pillars: the defence of EGLF, and the defence of the territoriality regime. The contributions to this volume reflect this double recommendation and focus on either or both pillars. First, a number of contributors (Sue Wright, Stephen May, Denise Réaume and David Robichaud) focus on the defence of English for non-identity purposes, such as enabling global democracy and global justice.

To begin with, Sue Wright's paper 'What is a Language?' invokes some of the recent research in sociolinguistics on English as a Lingua Franca, 'languaging' and superdiversity to criticize Van Parijs's defence of English. She makes a distinction between two ways of understanding English as a Lingua Franca, and supports the second. On the first, English as a Lingua Franca is understood as a language system. On the second, it is understood as a practice, according to which negotiation of meaning and recalibration in response to interlocutors is important. She argues that this alternative understanding of English as a lingua franca makes Van Parijs's attribution of distributive and cooperative injustice to the use of English as a lingua franca less convincing. Since English is used in new ways, native speaker norms do not necessarily prevail on this view, and the opposition is rather between those who do and those who do not master the practice understanding of language.

She also points to the existence of superdiversity within states to point out that there is no reason to think that the language used will be the territorially supported language, nor that it should be. Instead, speakers will employ flexibility and dialogical strategies of negotiation to find mutual ground. This will often involve a form of English as a lingua franca and other languages depending on the first languages of the speakers.

Like Wright, Stephen May also brings sociolinguistics to the table. He regrets that Van Parijs does not more clearly engage with the work on language and identity that has been going on in sociolinguistics. This shows for example, says May, in Van Parijs's purely communicative understanding of language, which neglects identity-based dimensions.

It is also at work in Van Parijs's understanding of a diglossia composed of English for wider communication and a local language. Sociolinguistic research has shown that in diglossic situations, the local language is inevitably seen as delimited and unhelpful, both by its speakers and by others. The result is that the local language tends to dwindle: in the real world, the notion of *stable* diglossia is a fiction.

Another area of research in sociolinguistics that Van Parijs ignores is the multiplicity of English. May criticizes Van Parijs for working with a monolithic and hegemonic view of English. Rather than just being one thing, there are various *Englishes*, such as Indian English or Malay English. And it is in fact only the high-status forms of English that may bring upward mobility for speakers. This is another reason why diglossia entrenches rather than reduces existing hierarchies. Since it is the existing elite that profits from English, Van Parijs's distributive justice case for English is flawed.

May also criticizes the territoriality principle, because it only caters to national minorities who have some territorial majority, thereby neglecting immigrant languages or languages without such a territorial dominance like Occitan, Breton and Frisian.

Whereas Sue Wright and Stephen May work out sociolinguistically inspired critiques of the defence of English, Denise Réaume and David Robichaud tackle the normative, politico-philosophical argument that Van Parijs articulates. In 'Lingua Franca Fever: Skeptical Remarks', Denise Réaume takes issue with three steps in Van Parijs's argument: the reasons for the emergence of English as a lingua franca, the reasons for supporting English, and the case for territoriality. Regarding the first, she argues that pre-existing conditions of power inequality are responsible for the coming-about of English as a lingua franca: the dominance of English stems from the economic, political and cultural power of, first, the British Empire and later the American Empire. Van Parijs may be right about the importance of probability-sensitive learning and the maximin rule, but the reason why these favour English is simply the result of the power that the English-speaking nations have exercised over the world. This casts the unfairness in a new light. If an unfair situation might not exist if not for unjust power relations, then treating it as inevitable will make its emergence a foregone conclusion. It is not clear that we should then just proceed and compensate as much as possible for the unfairness.

Réaume also challenges the two normative arguments for English: democracy and equality. The democracy argument states that a true deliberative democracy requires one shared language. But Réaume argues that this is too demanding. Instead it suffices if a relatively small minority in each language group is bilingual or multilingual. They could then translate political arguments between language groups. The egalitarian argument states that ensuring everyone speaks English is the best way to prevent a situation whereby only economically advantaged parents can get their children language training. But Réaume argues that advocating English as a means of reaching equality is not going to help because advantaged parents will then ensure that their children simply know English better by sending them to the best schools and so on. So the only thing that would help is to ensure that everyone speaks English just about as well as native speakers do, which is a very ambitious goal. Moreover, since the vast majority of people still live in their own language group, it seems overkill to give everyone lingua franca knowledge.

Finally, she argues that the territorial solution for languages is misguided because it uses local dominance to make up for the fact that another language has the upper hand in all inter-group interactions. We cannot solve the problem of unequal transnational status by giving each group equal national status. The central asymmetry between native speakers of English and others remains.

David Robichaud zooms in on Van Parijs's argument about the cooperative injustice of English, Van Parijs's second of the three sources of injustice ensuing from the lingua franca that he discusses in the book (apart from distributive injustice and esteem injustice). Van Parijs understands the cooperative injustice of English in the following way: all non-native speakers of English will learn English as a second language but the native speakers of English do not have to learn a second language. As a result, the non-natives do all the work and the native speakers free ride upon the efforts of the others.

Robichaud sets out to show, however, that the benefits that accrue to the native speakers of English cannot be seen as resulting from freeriding. In his view, cooperative benefits result from an agreement to cooperate. Free riders are people who agree to cooperate but then back down and act contrary to the agreement in the interest of their private concerns. The agreement is crucial. Without it, we could force unsuspecting others into cooperation and accuse them of injustice if they refuse to do so. So there is no a priori duty to cooperate.

Robichaud does not argue that people need to explicitly agree to the cooperation. It would be sufficient to be able to show that a situation without cooperation, where each party strives for his self-interest, would be disadvantageous for them, such that cooperation improves the situation of all. So showing that Anglophones benefit from the world learning English is not enough to conclude that there is cooperation to which Anglophones have a duty to contribute. We would need to show that everyone cooperated in a way that transcends their non-cooperative self-interest. If it is rationally advantageous for the non-native speakers to learn English, as is suggested by Van Parijs since he believes the spread of English is irreversible, then, since no compensation is needed by the native speakers to make it rationally advantageous – it already is advantageous for them in the absence of cooperative agreement – the native speakers are not freeriding.

So far we focused on Van Parijs's arguments for supporting English as the global lingua franca and remedying the injustices that occur in its wake. Now, we move on to the second normative pillar of Van Parijs's theory: his advocacy of the territoriality regime. In Van Parijs's view, language groups are allowed to 'grab a territory' on which their language can become the sole language of public institutions. He defends this regime on the basis of the normative importance of the identity interest in dignity, or esteem, which should be equally provided. Anna Stilz, Jean Laponce, Daniel Weinstock and Rainer Bauböck raise questions in this regard.

In her paper entitled 'Language, Dignity and Territory', Anna Stilz zooms in on Van Parijs's argument for invoking equality of dignity as an injustice that English inflicts upon the non-English world. Van Parijs claims that to systematically expect native speakers of another language to address English native speakers in English can legitimately be understood by the former as an insult. Stilz claims though since the choice for English is essentially driven by the possibility to have an as large as possible group of people to communicate with, we cannot assume that linguistic superiority is involved when native speakers of English communicate with others. It may be the case that people come to feel the use of English by the native speakers as disrespectful. But a feeling of disrespect does not necessarily ground reasonable claims: people may have feelings of disrespect about all sorts of practices that are not objectionable. To distinguish between unreasonable and reasonable claims, Stilz proposes a general criterion: it is reasonable to feel insulted by the choice of a social standard only where background power inequalities between groups have caused the particular shape of the social standard. The problem with English is then not that it is a standard perceived as insulting but that it is a standard that has emerged because a powerful group – the Anglophone countries – have imposed their will through superior power means. So with this background, power inequality criterion Stilz distinguishes reasonable from unreasonable claims to equal dignity and thus provides one way of substantiating Van Parijs's equal dignity claim.

She then goes on to argue that the linguistic territoriality principle as defended by Van Parijs is not a good way to realize the equal linguistic dignity claim because minorities might end up trapped within the linguistic territories. Instead, she proposes a least cost model for language policy, which starts from a multilingual policy but accepts that states have reason to impose some rationalization in a common language where that rationalization serves compelling public purposes such as economic opportunity or democratic participation. This can for example lead to a policy where a common language is promoted alongside policies that express the equal standing of the diverse linguistic minorities.

Van Parijs often speaks with respect of Jean Laponce, the inventor of what Van Parijs has termed the 'Laponce mechanism'. The mechanism is based on the insight of Laponce that 'the nicer people are with one another, the nastier languages are', which leads to assimilation pressures from dominant to weaker languages. This Laponce mechanism is for Van Parijs a central reason for endorsing the territoriality regime, as Laponce himself has done before. In his response to Van Parijs in this volume, Laponce by and large agrees with Van Parijs's invocation of his theory to ground territoriality, be it with several caveats.

Laponce agrees with Van Parijs that aiding the case of English is desirable. But because many do not speak English as a first language in the world, and because the level of one's knowledge of English matters for social stratification, he argues that English is not advantageous to all. With Van Parijs, Laponce also agrees that a minority language is best protected by coercive territorial authorities. But he differs with Van Parijs on territoriality in two ways. First he makes the language protection dependent on the condition that the authorities of the language community are of 'good international citizenship'. And second, he argues that referenda rather than 'objective' censuses should be used to solve or at least reduce intra-territorial language conflicts, such that some parts of the territory would be allowed to split from the rest of the territory if it votes differently. Finally, Laponce argues that language protection is to be grounded in the right to self-determination, rather than in Van Parijs's preferred parity of esteem.

In 'Can Parity of Self-Esteem Serve as the Basis of the Principle of Linguistic Territoriality?', Daniel Weinstock takes issue with Van Parijs's justification of the territoriality principle. He first argues that the parity of esteem argument cannot ground the coercive nature of the principle. To show the injustice of a situation, it does not suffice to point to feelings of lack of esteem. One would need to be able to show that a particular institutional setting is responsible for the lack of esteem. Moreover, many instances of assimilation pressure do not result from lack of esteem but from 'mere numbers': in mere numbers cases, the assimilation pressure ensues from the simple fact that one of the languages has the greatest number of speakers. While Weinstock thus questions the parity of esteem grounding, he still allows for instantiations of a liberal territoriality principle. Like Laponce, however, he argues that the territoriality principle can better be grounded in the value of democracy and self-determination: just like a group can decide to invest more or less in public services like libraries, it could decide to invest in language protection, provided liberal-democratic limits are respected.

Secondly, he argues that even the coercive version of the territoriality principle proposed by Van Parijs cannot influence language use in such a way that the language that benefits from the principle will no longer be assimilated by another language. Much more illiberal measures would be needed for that, such as initiatives to prevent native speakers from vulnerable languages from accessing stronger languages through the educational system.

In 'The political value of languages', Rainer Bauböck argues that parity of esteem fails as a justification for a coercive principle of territoriality. It fails because it cannot itself generate a criterion for deciding which languages will be protected by the principle and which will not be. We need such a criterion because there are many more languages than territories. But the parity of esteem argument cannot provide such a criterion because any language group can claim equal esteem.

Like Laponce and Weinstock, Bauböck instead argues that the (coercive) territoriality principle can be directly grounded in the value of self-government and democracy. Language is not only of value for individuals but also for collectives, because it provides territorial groups with boundaries and enables them to develop a shared public sphere. Bauböck's justification of territoriality then lies in the role of linguistic territoriality in securing self-government. The only test we can have for the legitimacy of language laws consists in verifying that those laws result from the legitimate exercise of self-government.

The structure of this collection is as follows: this introduction is followed by the eight critical responses mentioned above – the first four focusing on the proposal for English as a lingua franca, the latter four focusing on the proposal of the territoriality regime. The collection concludes with a lengthy reply by Van Parijs to the eight responses to his work.

Disclosure statement

No potential conflict of interest was reported by the authors.

Notes on contributors

Helder De Schutter is Associate Professor of Social and Political Philosophy at Katholieke Universiteit Leuven. He works on linguistic justice, federalism and nationalism. He has held visiting positions at Princeton University in 2006 and 2013–2014 and at the University of Oxford (Nuffield College) in 2008–2009. He is also a guest professor at the Université Saint-Louis – Bruxelles. Previous publications have appeared in journals and books including *British Journal of Political Science, Inquiry, The Journal of Political Philosophy, Journal of Applied Philosophy, Metaphilosophy, CRISPP, Nationalities Papers, Politics, Philosophy, and Economics* and *The Cambridge Companion to Language Policy* (2012).

David Robichaud is Associate Professor in Moral and Political Philosophy at the University of Ottawa and a member of the Groupe de Recherche Interuniversitaire sur la Normativité (GRIN). Publications on trust, on linguistic justice and on social justice have appeared in a number of collective books including *The Cambridge Companion to Language Policy* (2012) and in journals such as *Philosophiques, Éthique publique, Journal of Multilingual and Multicultural development* and *Les ateliers de l'éthique*. He also published a book, *La juste part* (2012), and co-edited *Penser les institutions* (2013). He is co-editor of the online journal *Ethics and Economics*.

LINGUISTIC JUSTICE

References

Barro, R.J., 1996. *Getting it right*. Cambridge, MA: MIT Press.

Barry, B., 2001. *Cultural and equality. An egalitarian critique of multiculturalism*. Cambridge: Polity Press.

Carens, J., 2000. *Culture, citizenship and community. A contextual exploration of justice as evenhandedness*. Oxford: Oxford University Press.

Gadamer, H.G., 1975. *Truth and method*. London: Sheed & Ward.

Gadamer, H.G., 1976. *Philosophical hermeneutics*. Berkeley, CA: University of California Press.

Gans, C., 2003. *The limits of nationalism*. Cambridge: Cambridge University Press.

Ginsburgh, V. and Weber, S., 2011. *How many languages do we need?* Princeton: Princeton University Press.

Grin, F., 2006. Economic considerations. *In*: T. Ricento, ed. *An introduction to language policy theory and method*. Oxford: Blackwell, 77–94.

Herder, J.G., 1877–1913. *Sämtliche Werke*, ed. B. Suphan, 33 vols. Berlin: Weidmann Verlag.

Huntington, S., 2004. *Who are we? The challenges to America's national identity*. New York: Simon and Schuster.

Kukathas, C., 2003. *The liberal archipelago*. Oxford: Oxford University Press.

Kymlicka, W., 1995. *Multicultural citizenship. A liberal theory of minority rights*. Oxford: Oxford University Press.

Kymlicka, W. and Patten, A., eds., 2003. *Language rights and political theory*. Oxford: Oxford University Press.

Laponce, J., 1987. *Languages and their territories*. Toronto, ON: University of Toronto Press.

Margalit, A. and Raz, J., 1995. National self-determination. *In*: W. Kymlicka, ed. *The rights of minority cultures*. Oxford: Oxford University Press.

Miller, D., 1995. *On nationality*. Oxford: Oxford University Press.

Moore, M., 2001. Normative justifications for liberal nationalism: justice, democracy and national identity. *Nations and nationalism*, 7 (1), 1–20.

Musschenga, A., 1998. Intrinsic value as a reason for the preservation of minority cultures. *Ethical theory and moral practice*, 1, 201–225.

Patten, A., 2001. Political theory and language policy. *Political theory*, 29 (5), 683–707.

Patten, A., 2003. Liberal neutrality and language policy. *Philosophy & public affairs*, 31 (4): 356–386.

Patten, A., 2014. *Equal recognition. The moral foundations of minority rights*. Princeton: Princeton University Press.

Pogge, T., 2003. Accommodation rights for hispanics in the U.S. *In*: W. Kymlicka and A. Patten, eds. *Language rights and political theory*. Oxford: University Press, 105–122.

Rawls, J., 1996. *Political liberalism*. New York: Columbia University Press.

Rawls, J., 1999. *A theory of justice*. Cambridge, MA: Harvard University Press.

Raz, J., 1995. *Ethics in the public domain*. Oxford: Oxford University Press.

Réaume, D., 2003. Beyond personality: the territorial and personal principles of language policy reconsidered. *In*: W. Kymlicka and A. Patten, eds. *Language rights and political theory*. Oxford: Oxford University Press, 271–295.

Rockefeller, S.C., 1994. Comment. *In*: A. Gutmann, ed. *Multiculturalism and the politics of recognition*. Princeton: Princeton University Press, 87–98.

Stilz, A., 2009. Civic nationalism and language policy. *Philosophy & public affairs*, 37 (3), 257–292.

Tamir, Y., 1995. *Liberal nationalism*. Princeton: Princeton University Press.

Taylor, C., 1993. Reconciling the solitudes. Essays on Canadian federalism and nationalism. *In*: Guy Laforest, ed. Montréal: McGill-Queen's University Press.

Taylor, C., 1994. The politics of recognition. *In*: A. Gutmann, ed. *Multiculturalism and the politics of recognition*. Princeton: Princeton University Press, 25–73.

Van Parijs, P., 2011. *Linguistic justice for Europe & for the world*. Oxford: Oxford University Press.

Weinstock, D., 2003. The antinomy of language rights. *In*: W. Kymlicka and A. Patten, eds. *Language rights and political theory*. Oxford: University Press, 250–270.

What is language? A response to Philippe Van Parijs

Sue Wright

Centre for European and International Studies Research, University of Portsmouth, Portsmouth, UK

When we consider the issue of linguistic justice, we must define what we mean by language. Standardisation of languages is closely associated with the development of the nation state, and the de Saussurian conception of language as system is in concert with nationalism and its divisions. In the early twenty-first century, however, this view of the world as a mosaic of stable national monolingualisms is outdated. In a globalising world, much of the political, social and economic structure that is developing is transnational and patterns of contact, both real and virtual, have become extraordinarily complex. In the resulting communities of communication of this superdiverse world, much language practice is more function driven than in the recent past. New practices mean that we cannot consider questions of linguistic justice in this new world order using the linguistic toolkit of the old. The flows, exchanges and networks of globalisation present us with a new paradigm and we need to recalibrate concepts.

Introduction

It is extremely useful to strip the debate about language attitudes, choices and practices back to bare essentials. In doing this, professor van Parijs gives us an insightful analysis of current concerns which cuts through much of the obfuscation that habitually cloaks language issues and masks group interests and rivalries. There is, however, one element in the mix, which he does not examine forensically, and that is language itself. In my response to his book, I would thus like to concentrate on this aspect and deconstruct what we mean by language. I am going to argue that it is essential to define our understanding of the nature of language before we pass to a discussion of how to encourage justice in the linguistic domain.

This understanding is deeply rooted in social and political contexts. How we view language is not a given, fixed once and for all. In my response, I am going to take a 'longue durée' view and address the historical dimension of the issue and show how much political, social and economic contexts determine language attitudes and behaviour.

27

What is a language?

In scholarship, there have been two divergent positions on the nature of language. The first derives from the scientific tradition that holds that there is a 'real' world 'out there' that can be understood and described objectively in language. It finds expression in positivism in the nineteenth century and some strands of structuralism in the twentieth century. The second is rooted in the belief that speakers/writers are autonomous subjects who, through free will, co-construct meaning with their interlocutors. From nineteenth century, romanticism to late twentieth post-modernism, scholars in this tradition argue that individuals create language from their own life experiences and for their own personal communicative needs. For the first group, language is used to describe reality and, for the second, language frames that reality.

Halliday has defined these two quite distinct and oppositional traditions as philosophical–logical and descriptive–ethnographic:

> In the former, linguistics is part of philosophy and grammar part of logic; in the latter, linguistics is part of anthropology and grammar is part of culture. The former stresses analogy; is prescriptive, or normative, in orientation; and concerned with meaning in relation to rhetorical function. The former sees language as thought; the latter sees language as action. The former represents language as rules ... The latter represents language as choices or as resource. (Halliday 2003, pp. 99–100)

An understanding of this dichotomy is a prerequisite for any useful discussion of language rights. It affects what we mean when we say, for example, that we want to promote 'parity of esteem' (van Parijs 2011, p. 174) for different 'languages'. Do we mean that we wish to preserve an ideal system, a free-standing structure or do we mean that we are setting out to safeguard the rights of speakers to maintain their practices? Before any attempt at language management, we have to ask: 'Do we believe language to exist apart from its speakers or do we conceive language as ongoing and ever-changing social behaviour?' Whether we consider language as autonomous system or as dialogic creativity, as rules or resource profoundly affects how we approach the whole question of linguistic justice.

Language as system and nation-building

The concept of language as strictly ordered system is closely connected with the growth of the nation state in Europe. This kind of political arrangement seemed to need a codified standardised form of language for its development. Standard languages and homogenised groups on defined territory developed in tandem.

In the early modern period, monarchs began to wrest power from their barons and rule through a centralised administration. Their fledgling bureaucracies and legal systems functioned in the language of the king and the capital. In concert, the phenomenal growth of print in the 16th and 17th centuries promoted the standardisation and spread of this single medium.

And when rebellion and revolution challenged the absolute power of the monarch, the process of standardising language and promoting this single standard gained impetus. If the people were to replace the monarch as the locus of sovereignty and legitimacy then there needed to be a means of consulting them. Subjects and citizens have different communication needs: the former can be 'told' and this can be accomplished through bilingual intermediaries; the latter must be 'consulted' and this provokes the need for a community of communication. Thus, the status, corpus and acquisition planning necessary to achieve a homogenous community of communication became part and parcel of nation-building. And every national group aspiring to self-determination and a national homeland undertook such language planning at an early stage in its mobilisation (Wright 2004).

Other technical and social developments underpinned the linguistic homogenisation of the national group: industrialisation required a more educated population (Gellner 1983) and state education systems provided the training, thus ensuring spread of the national language; the growing consumption of mass media in the national language (Anderson 1991) promoted competence in both written and spoken forms of the national language; citizen armies replaced mercenary forces and general conscription brought together the young men of the national group with inevitable consequences for linguistic convergence (Walter 1988).

Linguists contributed to the ideology that language is a strictly ordered system and that language use, national group and national territory should ideally be congruent (the fundamental European ideology of one language, one people, one state). As they codified and standardised the national language (often working in national language academies), applied linguists strove to provide the linguistic underpinning to national claims to be unique and separate. This was not self-evident as only the speakers of the pre-Indo-European language (Basque), the Finno-Ugric languages (Finnish, Estonian and Hungarian) and the Indo-European isolate (Albanian) could easily use language as a boundary marker. Most Europeans spoke languages which belonged to dialect continua (Romance, Germanic, Slavic, etc.), and at the beginning of the modern period, the linguistic landscape is best described as overlapping isoglosses with no clear linguistic demarcation lines on the continuum. The boundaries came as linguists engaged in what Kloss (1967) termed *Ausbau*. As national languages were codified and standardised, the aim was to achieve maximum linguistic convergence within the national group and maximum linguistic differentiation from other neighbouring (national) groups (Milroy and Milroy 1985).

Theoretical linguistics was in concert with the political imperatives of nation-building. De Saussure's seminal work directed attention to the discrepancies between language systems as they are described in grammar books and dictionaries and taught in formal education and actual language practices. He developed a description where language is divided between *langue* and *parole*, where the latter is the performance of individual speakers with all the idiosyncracies of their idiolects and is an imperfect and incomplete reflection of the former, which is the ideal system.[1] De Saussure himself does not go so far as to claim that language has a life of its own. His view is more subtle: *langue*, the ideal system, cannot be witnessed in its entirety in the repertoire of any speaker; *langue* exists perfectly only within the collectivity (de Saussure 1916, p. 14). But, although he would have argued that language cannot be reified and seen as existing independently of speakers, he did conceive it as an imagined system that represents the totality of what all its speakers do. And as his ideas spread, this subtlety was mostly neglected. Out of context, his famous quote 'Language is speech less speaking' (de Saussure 1916, p. 77) seems to formally endorse the idea of perfect system.

An influential strand of twentieth century linguistics followed in this mould, focusing on internal logical or grammatical mechanisms. Hjemslev and the school of glossematics 'took the Saussurean dictum that langue is form not substance to its logical conclusion' (Harris 2001, p. 128) and worked in the sphere of possible and ideal systems rather than naturally occurring language. Chomsky (1968, p. 111) set out to 'abstract away from conditions of use of language and consider formal structures and the formal operations that relate them'. Generative linguistics was concerned with the ideal native speaker, rather than actual practice.

The legacy of structuralism with its idea of language as an abstract, self-contained conceptual system, a system of incontestable, normatively identical forms is extremely powerful. In the vast majority of cases, Europeans are still socialised and schooled in one national language and taught to respect a rule-based system. When and if they learn another language in school, this is billed as 'foreign' and requires acquisition of another set of rules. How most Europeans view language is caught perfectly by the metaphor van Parijs borrows from Gellner (1983), who compared the European nation state language system to a Modigliani painting where boundaries are clearly demarcated. Europeans have been taught to see their languages as discrete and to downplay the resemblances between neighbours on the dialect continua.

The Modigliani metaphor applies not only to language but also to much political, social, economic and cultural activity in the nation state system. Europe of the nation states can be seen as a 'mosaic', with each interlocking national piece maintaining clear boundaries. Within national frontiers, national sovereignty was inviolable; no law superseded national law; the domestic market was protected; the national currency independent; national defence was assured by a national army; national media broadcast to the nation in the national language, national education systems socialised the young into the national system, culture was largely a national affair. To use a different metaphor, we could describe nation states as 'containers', in each of which national life was played out in the national language. When national members exited their container, they entered *alien* systems, using *foreign* languages.

It seems to me that it is this concept of language and group that underpins van Parijs' analyses of linguistic justice as fair cooperation (van Parijs 2011, pp. 50–85) and as equal opportunity (van Parijs 87–113). In his exploration of language injustices, there is the underlying assumption that we are dealing with homogenous national groups using discrete national language systems. When he considers the possibility of some kind of tax transfer from one national linguistic group to another to redress the imbalances of linguistic advantage/disadvantage, it is clear that he has the self-contained system concept of national languages in mind. Thus, if there is any evidence to support the idea that clearly demarcated political and linguistic systems are undergoing change (i.e. that they were actually a construct of Modernity rather than fundamental and unchanging structures), then van Parijs' analysis of linguistic relationships becomes outmoded.

Language as practice and a globalising world

So what evidence is there that our understanding of the world as compartmentalised states and discrete language systems is undergoing change? First, we can argue that the nation state system has weakened. Although it is clear that the nation state is still far from extinct, every factor (national sovereignty, market, defence, cultural homogeneity, media and infrastructure) that characterised it has undergone or is undergoing some modification.[2] In Europe, change has been far-reaching:

- Some national *sovereignty* has been relinquished as governments have signed the various treaties of the European Union and the various charters of the Council of Europe. Some supranational commercial law and some international human rights law regularly take precedence over national laws.
- The protected domestic *market* has been replaced by the European common market, which itself is operating within a world system where the pressure is to move to neo-liberal free market practice. In addition, transnational corporations escape the control of the nation state and work on a world stage to avoid control and tax.
- National *defence* is now enmeshed in larger systems. Most European states are part of NATO and rely on fellow members in a contract that is more binding than old style alliances. The doctrine of non-interference in the internal affairs of states is increasingly challenged.[3]
- *Transport* infrastructure allows movements across boundaries for relatively low cost and effort. And there are fewer formalities. Under the Schengen agreement, most European states have relinquished border passport controls.

- Cultural heterogeneity has replaced the fleeting and precarious homo-geneity achieved within the nation state. Migration from former colonies brought millions to Europe in the second half of the twentieth century. The Treaty on European Union (1992) increased labour mobility within the EU. And even where stringent immigration control has been (re-)introduced, governments have not been able to stem flows which have continued on clandestine routes. The result is diverse and complex migrant communities, particularly in the major cities. The *assimilatory pressures* that the national host communities attempt to exert may have little effect in such settings.
- E-technologies are democratising both access to information and its pub-lication. National audio-visual and print *media* are increasingly supple-mented (if not replaced) by internet networks where news circulates transnationally and with little regard to 'authorities' and hierarchies.

Given the change in each of these political, economic and social contexts, the key contexts that shaped and maintained national language systems, we should expect linguistic developments. All the changes listed above involve people in various kinds of linguistic border crossing, and we can see new communities of communication forming in the flows, exchanges and networks of this increasingly trans-national world. As van Parijs (2011, pp. 21–37) notes, the increasingly common solution is to use English to participate in globalisation. The question then arises what we mean by the term 'English'.

Are these border-crossing communications taking place in the codified, standardised national language used in the UK, the US, Canada or Australia, etc. or is some new linguistic development taking place? In van Parijs' argument, there is a tendency to assume the former. In some respects, he is accurate. Much elite language use in international settings is still standard UK or US English. The written standard continues to be the norm in most formal publication (e.g. scientific research, legal documents etc.). Alongside the native speakers, those who have expended the considerable effort and expense of acquiring standard UK and US Englishes continue to use them. They are cultural capital in Bourdieu's (1982) sense of the term and mastery of these standards still confers prestige in some circles.

However, this is a fluid situation. In the long term, it is unlikely that communities of communication using English as a lingua franca (ELF) will con-tinue to be shaped by the standard of native speakers. Intelligibility and commu-nicative efficiency will be the benchmarks rather than the model of native speaker forms. Given the knowledge that we have in linguistics about language change in situations of language contact and about how language is developed to be fit for purpose, we should expect linguistic change when large numbers of non-native speakers of English regularly use it among themselves.[4] We should also be aware of how ELF is increasingly used in new contexts that are not policed or dominated by English native speakers. In new settings, for example, the virtual, ephemeral and unconstrained interaction of online social networks or the diverse complexities of the great megalopolises, it becomes increasingly difficult to recognise any cross linguistic interaction as obeying the strict rules of national language as system, and this is particularly true for English.

What is happening is not yet clear. A major debate is currently raging about the nature of ELF. In sociolinguistics, there is a clash between those who are amassing vast corpora in order to be able to track new patterns of ELF usage (e.g. House 2002, 2010, Mauranen 2003, Jenkins 2007, Seidlhofer 2011, 2012) and those who believe that such codification will encourage unhelpful standardisation and models (e.g. Saraceni 2008, 2009, 2010, Canagarajah 2013, Rubdy and Alsagoff 2013). There is some confusion over whether ELF is a new variety that can be described. Can ELF be seen as a set of norms and constraints? Can it be seen as a set of alternative models? Should it rather be conceived as an approach, where negotiation allows the mutual shaping of the language that will be used in that particular community of communication? The only thing that we can say with any certitude is that in the enormous, amorphous mass of ELF users, agency is bottom up rather than top-down; language form is less predictable and more flexible as users negotiate meaning to fit their purposes. There is tension; in order that communication succeeds, features need to be recognisable by the interlocutors but, without normative pressure, they are moulded in each individual instance of communication of ELF. Variants can be unproblematic where the interlocutors understand the need to negotiate meaning. Without processing, however, they may cause misunderstanding. It is disconcerting for those used to strict rules and guidelines in language, to understanding language as right or wrong, to find themselves in a position where language is more fluid.

Now as many aspects of national life take on a global dimension and actors in different sectors establish and manage transnational relationships, Halliday's (1978) term 'languaging' seems to encapsulate the creative process of accommodation and negotiation to be noted in some language interaction. Medvedev, Voloshinov and Bakhtin's [5] understanding that human language is essentially creative, and therefore inevitably divergent and tending to heterogeneity, provides a useful paradigm. The latter argued that a view of language that stresses structure and system to the detriment of creativity and negotiation of meaning does not reflect how language actually works.[6] Voloshinov framed the argument in the following way:

> (T)he task of understanding does not basically amount to recognizing the form used, but rather to understanding it in a particular, concrete context, to understanding its meaning in a particular utterance, i.e. it amounts to understanding its novelty and not to recognizing its identity. (Voloshinov 1994, p. 33)

So while understanding that we are in a process of change with all the attendant difficulties this causes for analysis, I think that it is still possible to claim that ELF is more accurately described as 'language in practice' than 'language as system'. ELF is characterised by negotiation of meaning, recalibration in response to interlocutors and a high degree of linguistic accommodation. The resulting dialogic creativity is often fit for purpose but may depart in varying degrees from norms recognised as English by native speakers. Such new language behaviours adopted in order to instigate and maintain relations across language borders undermine the old paradigm of second language acquisition where the aim was to learn a different national language system and acquire native speaker like mastery of a free-standing linguistic structure. If we accept this description of language which foregrounds creativity and adaptation and challenge the view of language as unified construct, what consequences does this move from 'language as system' to 'language as practice' have for van Parijs' linguistic justice argument?

English as a lingua franca: who is advantaged?

To start with, it affects the issue of 'advantage'. Focussing on Europe, van Parijs notes that a transnational elite is evolving in professional spheres as governance, law, research, commerce, etc. become increasingly European rather than national. He reports that highly mobile professionals working in supranational and international settings are increasingly using ELF. The development of a lingua franca is, he claims, a good thing and aids this collaboration, but there is a profound injustice implicit in the situation: those who acquire English as a second language to use in trans-, inter- and supra-national settings are providing a social good at high personal cost, which those who have acquired English as a first language have not had to pay. He reflects on the inequality in linguistic relationships which permits English native speakers in political, managerial or professional roles to rely on others' knowledge of English and to function in multilingual settings without effort on their part. He suggests various ways that English native speakers could redress (or could be made to redress) the situation. It is difficult to disagree with his argument if we accept all the premises.

However, I am going to argue that advantage and disadvantage with regard to ELF is perhaps not quite as clear cut as van Parijs asserts. If we cease viewing language as a discrete system learnt as such in the classroom and informed by grammars and dictionaries and see it rather as the negotiation of meaning in context, we realise that the native speaker is not necessarily the best equipped to achieve successful interaction in transnational settings. If we accept the Bakhtinian claim that every utterance is 'a responsive link in the continuous chain of other utterances which, in effect, constitute the continuity of human consciousness' (Morris 1994, p. 5) who are then the skilled communicators? Those monolingual native English speakers whose limited language experience encourages them to see any 'linguistic form as a fixed self-identical signal' (Voloshinov 1994, p. 33) or those English-speaking multilinguals who have been trained to see language as 'a changeable and adaptable sign' (Voloshinov 1994, p. 33)? If all utterances are dependent on the context in which they are produced, and on what precedes and follows them, it seems valid to claim that a multilingual who moves between systems will be better at negotiating meaning in ELF communication than a monolingual whose education has not alerted them to the arbitrary nature of the sign nor to the fact that language is essentially action in context.

I would argue that anyone who is a native English speaker and who has never undertaken any serious and sustained second/foreign language learning may theoretically possess the linguistic system that enables transnational interaction, but will almost always have little skill in the 'languaging' that is necessary. This is a finding from two sets of fieldwork I carried out in 1996 and 2006 (Wright 2000, 2007). I investigated patterns of spoken communication in the European Parliament, where English is increasingly used in an informal way as a lingua franca. The findings showed disadvantage and advantage were linked more closely to 'monolingualism versus multilingualism' than to 'English native speaker competence versus the rest'. MEPs divided in the following way:

- One set of native English-speaking MEPs functions well in an ELF setting and derives some advantage from their English native speaker status. However, they only have this advantage because they are language aware. They are alert to the linguistic practices and political traditions that are national and which have no place in the EP. They can accommodate linguistically, negotiate and co-construct meaning.
- Another set of native English speakers performs extremely poorly in the multilingual setting of the EP even though, in theory, they can work in their first language (usually their only language). This malfunction stems from an extremely rigid view of language; they use English as they would with a homogenous group of native speakers. They fail to understand the mediated dimension of communication in the EP. Their linguistic insensitivity obstructs accommodation and negotiation. They regularly misconstrue meaning and they often fail to get their own message across to their heterogeneous audience.
- Those with first languages other than English who have good ELF skills do well in the networks of the parliament. Their linguistic sensitivity, honed by their own apprenticeship, predisposes them to accommodation, recalibration and negotiation in their interactions. They tailor their communication to the audiences they want to reach and are skilled in processing the messages they receive. It is noteworthy that the ELF they employ is often very far from English native speaker norms but fit for purpose.
- Those with first languages other than English who are disadvantaged by the presence of English as a lingua franca in the EP are all those who do

not have the skills to use ELF effectively or at all. They are side-lined from much of the informal political process. They cannot lobby informally nor access unofficial networks of information and even where translation and interpretation are available they may miss some of the message.[7]

The various linguistic behaviours of this elite group where English is used in novel dialogic interaction and where native speaker norms do not necessarily prevail illustrate that it may be problematic to portray advantage connected to the spread of English simply in terms of native speakers of English versus those with other first languages (e.g. van Parijs 2011, p. 92). The opposition may rather be between those who have acquired the flexibility to deal with language as action and those who are imprisoned within their own language system, whether this is English or any other language. If this is so, then the free-riding problem is not quite as van Parijs describes.[8] All those contributing to successful cross linguistic border interaction appear to have invested in some form of linguistic education/training.

Now, it is obviously true that ELF is close to national standard English and many argue that English native speakers start from a privileged position vis-à-vis ELF (e.g. Gazzola and Grin 2013). We can agree that this is still the case when non-native speakers of English strive to maintain UK and US standard forms and address monolingual English speakers in a stable language variety that these latter can correctly and quickly decipher. But such speakers are, in Halliday's analysis, those who are oriented to the prescriptive and the normative, focused on rules and concerned with meaning in relation to rhetorical function. We see such stability among professional linguists in the EP, but in my fieldwork, I found the politicians to be far less form-focused. In debate and negotiation, language was action and resource, and meaning was negotiated. If interaction is dialogic creativity with speakers using linguistic repertoires to create meaning in context, then, without the toolbox to appropriate, calibrate, repair and re-present, the monolingual is not privileged. To get the skills and perspective necessary to deal effectively with ELF interaction, it seems essential to acquire the linguistic awareness that comes with second language acquisition.

So to sum up, advantage seems to depend on how we conceive language. If we conceive language as stable system, we have the scenario where groups A to Y have learnt the *standard* language of group Z so there can be intergroup communication. In this case group Z benefit without effort on their part. If we conceive language as practice the following scenario may be more accurate. Many in groups A to Y have learnt the language used by group Z, appropriate it and use it in different ways as a lingua franca among themselves and sometimes with group Z. Often it is much easier to leave the Zs out of the network or the contract, because it takes a little more effort to interact with the Zs, who in their vast majority do not always seem to understand the particularity of the lingua franca and the different approach needed to understand and make themselves understood in the lingua franca setting. As one francophone MEP said to me in a 2006 fieldwork interview 'Je comprends tout le monde [en anglais], sauf les Anglais' (Wright 2007). In this case, the benefit to group Z is not so clear-cut.

The unresolved nature of the global lingua franca introduces a whole new set of problems for van Parijs' desire to introduce redistributive justice at global level for unequal access to it.

Language and migration

There is another line of argument in *Linguistic Justice for Europe and for the World* where this issue of standard language is also pertinent. In the discussion of linguistic territoriality (van Parijs 2011, pp. 133–174), we are once again faced with the question 'what is a language?'

Since World War II migration has created sites of complex transnational interaction in Europe. There is increasing linguistic heterogeneity in many towns and cities. In his chapter on linguistic territoriality, van Parijs (2011, pp. 133–174) discusses how communication could be managed in such settings. He develops the argument that ELF is more likely to be tolerated/ accepted if it is corralled very strictly to international interchange among groups who have different first/official languages. He argues that migrants should not rely on ELF for communication needs within a state (2011, p. 134 and 144) and that, once resident, they should commit to knowledge and use of the official state language. To enforce this, he calls for 'a territorially differentiated coercive linguistic regime that makes it realistic to expect immigrants to learn weaker local languages' (2011, p. 174).

If we disentangle the different categories of migrant, it becomes clear that once again we need to contrast 'language as system' versus 'language as practice'. Some migrants are in a better position to acquire the state language than others. Those who stay long enough for their children to be educated and who have the status which allows them to apply for citizenship will be pulled into the language, territory, people nexus. A number of European states have introduced citizenship tests with language competence assessment for those applying for residency or naturalisation (Wright 2008). Such citizenship testing for the older generation together with schooling in the official language for the younger generation will contribute to a 'well-entrenched territorial regime' and migrants in this category are most likely to learn the standard national language.

The problem is that a large number of migrants will not be resident long enough for education to have an effect or for citizenship to be on offer. Because 'more people are now moving from more places, through more places, to more places' (Vertovec 2010, p. 86), linguistic integration is becoming ever harder to achieve.[9]

This is true where elite migrants are constantly moved from job to job within trans-national corporations or international institutions and where English is the language of the workplace. They can exploit the linguistic repertoires of their co-workers to save themselves the effort of learning the language of the space in which they live (often briefly). Van Parijs is right to castigate their arrogance, but at the same time, it is true that circumstances do not aid them to 'do the right thing'. They lack the two prerequisites essential for successful second language acquisition: the need to learn and the opportunity to practise. Of course, failing to learn the host language may be disadvantageous to them; as monolinguals in a multilingual environment, they will experience the same problems as the monolingual MEPs, lacking control of interactions, always beholden to someone else's understanding and unable to tailor their own contributions appropriately.

In the case of migrants in unskilled work and refugees, Vertovec's observations are even more pertinent. Many European cities and towns have experienced substantial migration from many varied countries of origin. Vertovec (2007) defines the resulting mix as superdiversity, the diversification of diversity. He maintains that current diversity cannot be understood in terms of multiculturalism or even post-multiculturalism; it is more complex and enmeshed. In his view, we are looking at fusion rather than the coexistence of different cultures. Blommaert (2010) agrees, contending that migrant communities even in relatively small towns are immensely complex and that social organisation and exchange is being reinvented in these contexts. Evidence is emerging to show how language and identities are in flux in superdiverse settings (Fanshawe and Sriskandarajah 2010, Blommaert and Rampton 2011).

Such superdiversity is not a favourable setting for van Parijs' 'well-entrenched territorial regime'. Again the two conditions for successful language acquisition are often absent. A number of elements limit the motivation to acquire the state language. There may be instability – among those in unskilled work and with the most precarious employment, transport infrastructure and the porous nature of borders make it easy to move on if conditions become difficult or if opportunities appear better elsewhere. There will be differential immigration statuses with varying entitlements and restrictions of rights – those with little or no stake in the state may have insufficient motivation to acquire its language. There may be no economic imperative – patterns of settlement may make it likely that employment is provided within the migrant community. But most importantly, in the complexity of the population mix, the language of the state may be just one of many languages regularly encountered, the opportunities to acquire it in its standard form may well be scarce and the imperative to do so may be absent.

On the issue of the opportunity to practise, Vertovec makes the point that civil integration is likely to be achieved through 'the acquisition and routinisation of everyday practices for getting on with others in the inherently fleeting encounters that comprise city life.' These include simple forms of

acknowledgement, acts of restricted helpfulness, types of personal consideration [and] courtesies (2007, p. 4). If such interaction takes place with the host
community, it promotes some knowledge of the state language, but, in
conditions of superdiversity, civil integration is most likely to take place with
other immigrants, and here, the medium is unlikely to be the standard national
language.

A personal anecdote provides an example of such non-standard communication. I recently spent a semester in a small university town in central
Finland as visiting professor. I often ate in a restaurant where the cook was
Turkish and the waiter Lebanese. The staff from the local bicycle shop
(Somali, Kenyan and Ethiopian), and local Finns also ate there. The conversations I listened to and sometimes took part in over a number of weeks were
exactly the 'simple forms of acknowledgement, acts of restricted helpfulness,
types of personal consideration [and] courtesies' that Vertovec imagines. We
used all the linguistic and paralinguistic resources at our disposal to make and
maintain contact and show friendliness. I was so fascinated that I kept a language log and, looking at the interactions, it is difficult to pigeonhole them as
any named language that has a published dictionary and a grammar, although
ELF was clearly part of the mix. It seemed to me I was clearly involved in
language as practice, in an example of the Hallidayan notion that people
exchange meanings by 'languaging.'

So in current migration, what languages and what forms of languages are
likely to be acquired? Who learns language as system and who acquires language as practice? There are, of course, still formal classes for economic
migrants and refugees, where the standard host language is taught, although
provision has decreased in the increasingly stringent economic conditions after
the economic crisis of 2008. Migrants whose stay is extended and whose children are in state schools will have greater opportunity to learn the national
standard. Migrants who apply for citizenship must learn the national standard
as a condition for acceptance.

On the other hand, the communication needs of many migrants do not
require the acquisition of national standards or any language as system. In
superdiversity, interaction is mostly language in practice. For example, it is
unlikely that when van Parijs evokes 'Ecuadorians or Moroccans speaking at
least some Spanish in Catalonia, or Pakistanis or Kosovars speaking at least
some English in Sweden' (van Parijs 2011, p. 159), the languages in question
are standard English or standard Spanish. Typically, the interaction will be
negotiated using linguistic repertoires that include these lingua francas, which
will not be in standard forms. Although this is my speculation in the case of
van Parijs' example, there is ample current research to support the assertion.[10]

Perhaps it is necessary to recognise that the imposition of the territoriality
principle may not be as easy as in the nation-building past. We should
remember that the success of top-down policies to impose a single national
standard on a territory was in part due to the fact that the top-down pressure

from elites worked in tandem with other social and economic phenomena (industrialisation, urbanisation) and was in concert with widespread acceptance of nationalist ideology and patriotic identity. In the megalopolises that I am describing, the top-down requirement to acquire a national standard does not dovetail with new social and economic phenomena (the e-technology revolution, fluid patterns of migration) and is not in concert with the global and local identities that many migrants assume (Sebba 2002, de Fina 2003 etc.).

Concluding remarks

Van Parijs' book gets to the very heart of the connection between language and power and plays an extremely useful role in getting us to review this relationship. He explores possibilities in a world where the nation state is no longer fully sovereign and where justice is increasingly conceived as a matter for humanity rather than the nation. However, while he adopts what could be seen as a post-national stance in his search for justice in linguistic matters, van Parijs does not engage with the post-national view of language. He has not taken into consideration that 'language as system' is not an absolute but merely a product of a political and social system at a given point in human history.

He is not totally wrong in maintaining a container view of language. Cultural capital still accrues to those who acquire native-like knowledge of a prestige language of wider diffusion, and in elite transnational contact there is still advantage for those who acquire and employ a 'foreign' language 'fluently'. Folk linguistics (c.f. Niedzielski and Preston 2000) show how the vast majority of people still take a purist stance. Scholars in the Chomskyan tradition continue to investigate language as formal system and work from the premise that there is an ideal native speaker. But we are in a period of change. Linguistic research[11] increasingly foregrounds the concept of function over form. After centuries of academic focus on standard and prescription we could call this trend in linguistics the descriptive turn.[12]

So, I would argue that any discussion of linguistic justice has to consider the interdependent relationship of political structure and language. Any attempt to undertake formal language management in the second decade of the twenty-first century needs to acknowledge that the way we think about language and the ways we use it are changing along with political, social and economic settings. Linguistic justice cannot be discussed only in terms of the relations of homogenous national groups speaking national languages. The analysis has to take into account how elite and mass linguistic behaviours are changing in the fluid conditions of globalisation, transnational interaction and superdiversity. And perhaps we need to recognise that top-down language intervention was a phenomenon of nation state building, reliant on (national) identity politics. In a globalising world, there may be no consensual acceptance of an authority competent to impose linguistic solutions, and this would be particularly true if its policies ran counter to social processes. Agreement on where we can employ lingua francas and the rules for their usage will of course emerge, but may well come from bottom-up language in practice and may be more fluid and less stable than language systems in national frameworks.

Disclosure statement

No potential conflict of interest was reported by the author.

Notes

1. Notebooks discovered in Geneva in 1996 (Joseph 2012) suggest that de Saussure's ideas were more complex than this. However, it is how de Saussure's work was understood and used in the twentieth century which is of interest here.
2. Of course, many people are experiencing these changes with deep unease; the ideologies of the nation state are deeply rooted. And although they may be increasingly aware that their political, social and economic structures are in flux, many are not yet fully reconciled to change and there is resistance. There could yet be a nationalist backlash. However, and particularly for the aspects that interest us here, I believe we can claim that many facets of our world are now post-national.
3. For example NATO intervention in Bosnia, in 1995–1996 with UN agreement.
4. We already understand some of the likely processes of transplantation, crossover, acculturation and nativisation from the research undertaken by World Englishes scholars (e.g. Kachru 1998).
5. There is much dispute over the authorship of individual works. I thus group them and recognise the creative nature of their collaboration 1919–1929.
6. Outside the communist world a parallel and equally robust rejection of structuralism was gaining ground in the work of Wittgenstein and Austin.
7. In simultaneous interpretation, it is estimated that only about 60% of the text of a speech can be rendered. Therefore interpreters act as filters, foregrounding certain aspects of information and suppressing others. There is inevitably delay in the circulation of European Parliament documentation as texts are translated into all 24 official languages. This is problematic where a swift response is required and advantages the users of languages whose versions appear first, particularly the groups whose languages are used for drafting.
8. The failure of monolinguals in the multilingual setting of the European parliament is readily observable. The interactional incompetence of monolingual English MEPS is one of the reasons that keep them out of networks and blocks relationships. The monolingual Estonian or Portuguese is hampered by relay interpreting, blocked by delays in translation or unable to lobby in private and in confidence. Both groups are ineffectual politicians.
9. Migration may not be proportionally greater than in past centuries, but it does have novel features. For example the nineteenth century immigrant from Europe to the United States did not tend to return. The goal was to settle. Transport made it expensive and costly to remain on the move.
10. See for example Arnaut et al. (2012), Blommaert and Rampton (2011), Blommaert et al. (2012) Kytölä (2012) and the conference presentations at the superdiversity conferences held in Copenhagen 2012, Jyväskylä 2013.
11. The functionalist school includes scholars such as Firth and Halliday. They showed how linguistic structure is associated with the realisation of social structure, in a process of mutual creativity (Halliday 1978). Halliday's notion that

people exchange meanings by 'languaging' suggests a more creative process than Chomsky's implementation of a rigid system dependent on explicit mechanisms for generating possible sentences. Functionalist insights were taken up in discourse analysis, where the modalities of languaging are explored. Coulthard and Sinclair sought ways of analysing communication above the level of the sentences and the phrase. Fairclough investigated the relationship between social change and changes in discourse.

12. And if we have any doubts about whether there is actually rejection of top-down, elite-led prescription and acceptance of more organic, bottom-up, mass-led language behaviours, we have only to consider dictionary making. Lexicography exemplifies the change precisely; it has become an investigation of what people actually do, rather than instruction on what they should be doing. The new technologies permit the collection and processing of billions of words and phrases gathered from all kinds of language making situations. Corpora based dictionaries now reflect usage as well as model it.

Notes on Contributor

Professor Sue Wright is the author of a number of works on the role of language in nation-building and transnational association, including *Community and Communication* (2000) and *Language Policy and Language Planning: from nationalism to globalisation* (2004/2015). She is series editor (together with Helen Kelly-Holmes) of Palgrave's *Language and Globalisation* book series and editor (together with Ulrich Ammon and Jeroen Darquennes) of *Sociolinguistica*.

References

Anderson, B., 1991. *Imagined communities*. London: Verso.

Arnaut, K., *et al.* eds., 2012. Language and superdiversities. *Diversities* [online], 14. Available from: www.unesco.org/shs/diversities/vol14/issue2/art1.

Blommaert, J., 2010. *The sociolinguistics of globalization*. Cambridge: Cambridge University Press.

Blommaert, J. and Rampton, B., 2011. Language and superdiversity. *Diversities* [online], 13 (2). Available from: www.unesco.org/shs/diversities/vol13/issue2/art1.

Blommaert, J., *et al.*, 2012. *Dangerous multilingualism*. Basingstoke: Palgrave Macmillan.

Bourdieu, P., 1982. *Ce que parler veut dire* [Language and symbolic power]. Paris: Fayard.

Canagarajah, S., 2013. *Translingual practice: global Englishes and cosmopolitan relations*. London: Routledge.

Chomsky, N., 1968. *Language and mind*. New York: Harcourt Brace.

Fanshawe, S. and Sriskandarajah, D., 2010. *'You can't put me in a box'. Super-diversity and the end of identity politics in Britain*. Institute for Public Policy Research. Available from: http://www.ippr.org/publications/you-cant-put-me-in-a-box-super-diversity-and-the-end-of-identity-politics-in-britain.

de Fina, A., 2003. *Identity in narrative: a study of immigrant discourse*. Amsterdam: John Benjamins.

Gazzola, M. and Grin, F., 2013. Is ELF more effective and fair than translation? An evaluation of the EU's multilingual regime. *International journal of applied linguistics*, 23 (1), 93–107.

Gellner, E., 1983. *Nations and nationalism*. Oxford: Blackwell.

LINGUISTIC JUSTICE

Halliday, M.A.K., 1978. An interpretation of the functional relationship between language and social structure. *In*: M.A.K. Halliday, ed. *Language as social semiotic*. London: Edward Arnold, 183–193.

Halliday, M., 2003. *On language and linguistics*. London: Continuum.

Harris, R., 2001. Linguistics after saussure. *In*: P. Cobley, ed. *Semiotics and linguistics*. London: Routledge, 118–133.

House, J., 2002. *Communicating in English as a lingua franca. In*: S. Foster-Cohen, T. Ruthenberg, and M.-L. Poschen, eds. *Eurosla yearbook*. Vol. 2. Amsterdam: Benjamins, 243–261.

House, J., 2010. The pragmatics of English as a lingua franca. *In*: A. Trosborg, ed. *Across languages and cultures*. Berlin: Mouton, 363–387.

Jenkins, J., 2007. *English as a lingua franca: attitude and identity*. Oxford: Oxford University Press.

Joseph, J., 2012. *Saussure*. Oxford: Oxford University Press.

Kachru, B., 1998. English as an Asian language. *Links & letters*, 5, 89–108.

Kloss, H., 1967. Abstand languages and Ausbau languages. *Anthropological linguistics*, 9, 90–101.

Kytölä, S., 2012. Multilingual web discussion forums: theoretical, practical and methodological issues. *In*: M. Sebba, S. Mahootian, and C. Jonsson, eds. *Language mixing and code-switching in writing: approaches to mixed-language written discourse*. London: Routledge, 106–127.

Mauranen, A., 2003. The corpus of English as lingua franca in academic settings. *TESOL quarterly*, 37 (3), 513–527.

Milroy, J. and Milroy, L., 1985. *Authority in language: investigating language prescription and standardisation*. London: Routledge.

Morris, P., ed., 1994. *The Bakhtin reader*. London: Arnold.

Niedzielski, N. and Preston, D., 2000. *Folk linguistics*. Berlin: Mouton de Gruyter.

van Parijs, P., 2011. *Linguistic justice for Europe and for the world*. Oxford: Oxford University Press.

Rubdy, R. and Alsagoff, L., eds., 2013. *The global-local interface, language choice and hybridity*. Clevedon: Multilingual Matters.

Saraceni, M., 2008. English as a lingua franca: between form and function. *English today*, 24 (2), 20–26.

Saraceni, M., 2009. Relocating English: towards a new paradigm for English in the world. *Language and intercultural communication*, 9 (3), 175–186.

Saraceni, M., 2010. *The relocation of English: shifting paradigms in a global era*. Basingstoke: Palgrave.

de Saussure, F., 1916. *Cours de linguistique générale* [Course in general linguistics]. Paris: Payot.

Sebba, M., 2002. 'Global' and 'Local' identities in the discourses of British-born Caribbeans. *International journal of bilingualism*, 6, 75–89.

Seidlhofer, B., 2011. *Understanding English as a lingua franca*. Oxford: Oxford University Press.

Seidlhofer, B., 2012. Corpora and English as a lingua franca. *In*: K. Hyland, M. Chau, and M. Handford, eds. *Corpus applications in applied linguistics*. London: Continuum, 135–149.

Vertovec, S., 2007. *New complexities of cohesion in Britain: super-diversity, transnationalism and civil integration*. London: Commission on Integration and Cohesion, HMSO.

Vertovec, S., 2010. Towards post-multiculturalism? Changing communities, conditions and contexts of diversity. *International social science journal*, 61, 83–95.

Voloshinov, V., 1994. Marxism and the philosophy of language. *In*: P. Morris, ed. *The Bakhtin reader*. London: Arnold, 26–37.

Walter, H., 1988. *Le français dans tous les sens*. Paris: Robert Laffont.

Wright, S., 2000. *Community and Communication: from nation building to European integration*. Clevedon: Multilingual Matters.

Wright, S., 2004/2015. *Language policy and language planning*. Basingstoke: Palgrave.

Wright, S., 2007. English in the European parliament: MEPs and their language repertoires. *Sociolinguistica*, 21, 151–151.

Wright, S., 2008. Citizenship tests in Europe. *International journal on multicultural societies*, 10 (1), 1–9.

The problem with English(es) and linguistic (in)justice. Addressing the limits of liberal egalitarian accounts of language

Stephen May

Faculty of Education, Te Puna Wananga, The University of Auckland, Auckland, New Zealand

No one speaks English, and everything's broken ... (Tom Waits: *Tom Traubert's Blues*)

Van Parijs's *Linguistic Justice for Europe and the World* furthers a nascent examination of multilingualism within political philosophy, drawing on continental European contexts where multilingualism is the norm. Van Parijs argues, in effect for linguistic cosmopolitanism via English as the current world language, and this seems ostensibly to be a considerable improvement on 'the untrammeled public monolingualism' of Anglo-American political theory. However, Van Parijs's account is flawed in four key respects. First, there is the fundamental problem of his reductionist account of language – by which language is viewed only in terms of its communicative uses and reach and not in relation to its symbolic and identity functions. Second is his simplistic advocacy of English as a global lingua franca, which ignores issues of power and inequality, along with related delimited access to *high-status* English language varieties. Third are the inherent limitations associated with his advocacy of linguistic territoriality, which recognizes state-sanctioned languages but little else, thus failing to mitigate existing linguistic hierarchies. Finally, the wider argument for English as a global lingua franca is inevitably underpinned by a monolithic/hegemonic view of English itself. This monolithic conception of English stands in contradistinction, not only to the actual plethora of Englis*hes* in the world today, but also, more importantly, to their widely varying status and use in furthering cross-communication and related notions of social and economic mobility. The latter thus fatally undermines Van Parijs's central argument linking social and economic mobility ineluctably to access to English.

Introduction

Linguistic Justice for Europe and the World (Van Parijs 2011) is an important book within political philosophy and I welcome the opportunity to comment on it – both in terms of the normative liberal egalitarian assumptions that underpin it, as well as the robustness and reach of these assumptions when viewed through a different disciplinary lens. To the latter task, I bring my own interdisciplinary grounding in sociology and sociolinguistics. In what follows, I freely acknowledge the systematicity, significance, and sophistication of Van Parijs' arguments in relation to language, the culmination of work he has been pursuing in this area over the last decade or so. Indeed, the significance of *Linguistic Justice* is precisely in providing us with a systematic account of the interrelationships between language, inclusion and mobility, and, in particular, their implications for furthering an egalitarian model of justice in a globalized world dominated by English.[1]

However, Van Parijs's (2011) contribution is also important for another reason. It furthers a nascent examination of multilingualism in relation to language rights, drawing on continental European contexts where multilingualism is the norm. Acknowledging the reality of multilingualism is ostensibly a considerable improvement on what I have elsewhere called 'the untrammeled public monolingualism' of Anglo-American political theory (May 2014a), which argues, in effect, for the active subjugation of all language varieties other than the recognized national language, particularly when the latter also happens to be English. This position is perhaps most clearly exemplified by Barry (2001), who asserts unequivocally that minority languages – that is, languages not otherwise recognized as public languages by the requisite nation-state – must be relinquished as the price of wider national citizenship, since their ongoing maintenance entrenches the cultural isolationism of minorities, delimits their social mobility, and undermines common understandings of the good life – what Barry terms 'the politics of solidarity' (2001, p. 300). As Barry concludes, 'the choice of solidarity with one's cultural group should not give rise to any sort of relative disadvantage, compared with participation in the mainstream [national] society' (2001, p. 95). This line of argument is also endorsed without reservation by other prominent Anglo-American political philosophers, most notably, Pogge (2003) and Laitin and Reich (2003), and since I have critiqued this broad liberal egalitarian consensus at length elsewhere (see May 2003, 2012, Ch. 6), I will not rehearse these arguments again here.

What European political philosophers, including Van Parijs, offer as a potentially (more) useful counterpoint to this untrammeled public monolingualism is the notion of linguistic cosmopolitanism. Linguistic cosmopolitanism acknowledges the limits of the national language/nation-state model in an increasingly globalized world dominated by English, arguing the need for greater communicative reach (invariably, via English) as a means of enhancing individual social and economic mobility and for achieving group-based social justice aims that extend beyond nation-state borders. This is an important theoretical development but, as I will argue in what follows, it does little *in practice* to subvert or undermine existing linguistic hierarchies, nor does it achieve its aim of greater linguistic (and associated social and economic) portability for today's 'global citizens'. The principal reason for this is that linguistic cosmopolitanism willfully ignores underlying issues of class and power, along with related delimited access to *high-status* English language varieties.

The problem with disciplinary constraints

With this in mind, let me now turn specifically to Van Parijs's arguments and what I believe to be their inherent limitations. My first and overarching criticism of Van Parijs's work might seem an unfair one – that it is (still) too rooted in normative political philosophy to be of much practical use in the complex, multilingual, and increasingly globalized world of the early twenty-first century. However, this is unfair only inasmuch as academic disciplinary boundaries are still taken to be the sine qua non of 'serious' scholarship. My point here is twofold: that only interdisciplinary – or, ideally, transdisciplinary – academic approaches can adequately address all the issues at hand and, relatedly, that such discussions must reflect the complexities of actual multilingual communities in widely differing contexts. In both these respects, Van Parijs's account is found singularly wanting. Van Parijs does draw on work in economics – most notably, via his use of the Simpson Index – to illustrate his normative points, reflecting his own interdisciplinary background in so doing. However, given his concerns with language, it is surprising, to say the least, that he almost entirely ignores the extensive literature in sociolinguistics that has, over the last 50 years, addressed in detail questions of linguistic identity, status, rights, and use in the formulation of language policies at local, national, and supranational levels, and similarly, the challenges and opportunities of addressing the linguistic complexities of multilingual communities in relation to the same (see, e.g. May 2004, 2012; Ricento 2006 for useful summaries).[2] Meanwhile, the normative assumptions that underpin his account – as with much work in political philosophy – remain primarily supported by hypothetical and/or abstract examples (although Van Parijs's penchant for anecdotal accounts is also much in evidence) rather than the more complex, nuanced empiricism that is actually needed to support such claims (May *et al.* 2004).

I address the specific implications of these disciplinary constraints in subsequent sections in four key respects. First, there is the fundamental problem of his reductionist account of language – by which language is viewed only in terms of its communicative uses and reach and not in relation to its symbolic and identity functions (cf. Rubio-Marín 2003, Bishop and Phillips 2006). This bifurcation of the instrumental and identity functions of language fails to account for, or explain, the latter's ongoing influence on language use and choice in the real world, at both individual and collective levels, nor does it provide a basis for ensuring the linguistic parity of esteem with which he is so concerned. Second is Van Parijs's related advocacy of English as a global lingua franca. This, in effect, endorses a form of international diglossia in which English serves the higher-level instrumental function of global interconnection and communicative exchange, while local/national languages are restricted to low(er) status, context-specific identity, and use functions. However, history shows us that diglossic contexts do little, if anything, to mitigate existing linguistic hierarchies, and their deleterious effects over time on lower status 'local' languages. Third, Van Parijs's advocacy of linguistic territoriality as the means of mitigating these linguistic hierarchies – and, in particular, the potential for English to usurp all other languages – is similarly found wanting. While his advocacy of territoriality, based on the European experience, does allow for public multilingualism, this is limited to state-sanctioned national languages and/or regional majority languages. Immigrant languages, associated language rights claims, and related hierarchies associated with public/private language use are entirely ignored. Finally, the wider argument for English as a global lingua franca is also inevitably underpinned by a monolithic/hegemonic view of English itself. This monolithic conception of English stands in contradistinction, not only to the actual plethora of English*es* in the world today, but also, more importantly, to their widely varying status and use(fulness) in furthering cross-communication and related notions of social and economic mobility. The latter, in particular, undermine a principal tenet of the arguments for linguistic cosmopolitanism – as exemplified by the likes of Van Parijs (see also de Swaan 2001, Archibugi 2005 and below) – that access to, and the opportunities afforded by, English will inevitably provide upward mobility and wider engagement with the world for those for whom English is not a first language (L1).

The limits of rational choice and instrumental accounts of language

In an earlier account that closely echoes Van Parijs's broad arguments, Abram de Swaan (2001) analyzes the relative reach and influence of languages in the world, along with their implications for governance and communication. In his analysis of this 'constellation' of world languages, de Swaan distinguishes and ranks languages on the basis of their 'Q value'. For de Swaan, the Q value or 'communication value' of a language is measured by combining the 'prevalence' of a language (the percentage of speakers of a language within the wider constellation of languages) with its 'centrality', that is the percentage of its *multilingual* speakers among all multilinguals in the constellation (2001, p. 178). Thus, the higher the Q value, the greater the communicative reach, significance, and usefulness of the language concerned. By this, de Swaan identifies 100 or so languages as 'central' (national languages, in effect). Twelve are identified as 'supercentral' (crossing national contexts): English, Arabic, Mandarin, Spanish, French, German, Hindi, Japanese, Malay, Portuguese, Russian, and Swahili. While only one, English, is 'hypercentral'.

Van Parijs comes to the same conclusion about the ascendancy of English but, in so doing, dispenses with de Swaan's notion of centrality. Rather, Van Parijs argues that prevalence alone is a sufficient indicator for the incontrovertible dominance of English as the current world language. It is on this basis that he outlines the argument for the adoption of English as the essential lingua franca for all speakers, especially for those who do not speak it as an L1. Two underlying principles are central to his argument here. The first is the principle of *probability-driven* learning, linking language learning and competence (with particular reference to English) to the projected extent of subsequent language use and the allied notions of *motivation* and *opportunity* (2011, p. 12). As he argues,

> the probability of interaction in a particular language can be regarded as the central determinant of the extent to which average competence in a particular non-native language tends to expand or shrink in a particular population. A greater probability means both a larger expected benefit from any given level of proficiency in the language concerned and a lower cost of acquiring or maintaining it. (2011, p. 13)

The growing perception of the essential need for English in 'a high mobility, intense-communication world' (2011, p. 23) thus reinforces probability-driven language learning – a broadly intrinsic characteristic, in effect, to opt to learn and use English as a lingua franca. Meanwhile, the need, particularly for multilingual speakers, to seek out a language that is most widely known by all participants in any communicative exchange provides an extrinsic pressure to opt for English as well, since English now boasts the greatest number of additional language learners of any language. Van Parijs terms the latter the *maxi-min* language principle (a development of his 'maximum law of communication' in his earlier work; see, e.g. 2004). This second underlying principle of opting for the language of maximal–minimal competence for any given number of speakers in order, as far as possible, to achieve effective communication with all participants again necessarily reinforces what he bluntly describes as the 'stampede towards English' (2011, p. 21). While Van Parijs acknowledges that there are exceptions to these principles, such as the deliberate privileging of one's own L1 for symbolic reasons, or the need to ensure against communicative breakdown in a language less well known by participants, the desire to communicate at the broadest/widest level trumps these considerations. This includes, for Van Parijs, contexts of demonstrably unequal power which may well (continue to) privilege L1 English speakers. And while these are not necessarily welcome, he concludes that they are nonetheless an unavoidable by-product of the maxi-min principle.

However, there are two fundamental problems with this analysis. The first is that Van Parijs's argument, along with that of other linguistic cosmopolitans, is predicated on the assumption that linguistic diversity is a *cost* which fundamentally militates against the accomplishment of social, economic, and linguistic justice precisely because it delimits the possibilities of effective communication (and thus deliberative democracy) in the first instance. Van Parijs uses the Simpson Index to measure linguistic diversity and the related notions of linguistic fragmentation and distance (the nomenclature itself reinforcing a negative comparison between diversity and communicative efficacy). In so doing, he again highlights their apparently obverse relationship to democratic justice at the collective level and to wider social and economic mobility at the individual level.

I will return to questions of language, justice, and mobility in due course. Let me here explore further the second key problem underlying his analysis – namely, that if language is only about communication then, *ipso facto*, the only concerns one should have about language relate to its communicative functions. Thus, the nod to the symbolic dimensions aside,[3] we are left with a highly reductive, instrumentalist view of language that ignores the historical associations that languages carry and, relatedly, their significance in relation to both individual and collective identities. Of course, this is not a particularly new intellectual position, and it extends well beyond the borders of Van Parijs's own grounding in economics and political philosophy. For example, from a sociological perspective, the idea that language(s) can be dissociated from identity and viewed in solely instrumentalist terms can be traced to the methodological individualism of rational choice theory. Methodological individualism, which was first applied in sociology to discussions of ethnic identities (see, e.g. Hechter 1986, Banton 1987), assumes that groups are constituted from individual behavior and are subject to continuous change as individuals respond to changing circumstances. In this view, social relations become a form of market relations with individuals making rational choices about their ethnic alignment(s) solely on the basis of the social and material gains it will bring them. This instrumentalist view was bolstered by a related social constructionist critique of ethnicity in both sociology and anthropology, beginning with Barth's (1969) *Ethnic Groups and Boundaries*, which has since consistently disavowed any intrinsic link between particular ethnic identities and specific cultural attributes. The 'cultural stuff' of ethnicity, as Barth puts it, may change, differ in salience in time, and in context, may simply come and go. They are not significant in themselves, only in relation to how they are deployed to distinguish one group from another.

Extrapolating these arguments to the question of language is relatively straightforward and thus also much in evidence in the sociolinguistics of the last 30 years or so. On this view, while a specific language may be identified as a significant cultural marker of a particular ethnic group, there is no inevitable correspondence between language and ethnicity. In effect, linguistic differences do not always correspond to ethnic ones – membership of an ethnic group does not necessarily entail an ongoing association with a particular language, either for individual members or for the group itself. Likewise, more than one ethnic group can share the same language while continuing without difficulty to maintain their own distinct ethnic (and national) identities. Even where language *is* regarded as a central feature of ethnic identity, it is the *diacritical significance* attached to language which is considered crucial, not the actual language itself (cf. Barth 1969). Moreover, languages, along with other cultural attributes, vary in their salience to ethnicity both within and between historical periods, and this also helps to explain why the association of particular languages with particular ethnic groups may well change over time. This, in turn, has been used within sociolinguistics to explain (and, at times, legitimize) processes of language shift and loss which have led both individuals and groups to abandon historically associated languages in favor of dominant national languages and, increasingly, international languages such as English (see, e.g. Edwards 1994, 2009, 2010, Brutt-Griffler 2002).

But taking this broader disciplinary view also allows us to critique more effectively its key limitations, something which Van Parijs's account singularly fails to do. For a start, to say that language is not an inevitable feature of identity is *not* the same as saying it is unimportant. Indeed, there is considerable evidence 'in the real world' that suggests that, while language may not be a *determining* feature of ethnic identity, it remains nonetheless a *significant* one in many instances. Or to put it another way, it simply does not reflect adequately, let alone explain, the heightened saliency of language issues in many historical and contemporary political conflicts, particularly at the intrastate level (see Weinstein 1983, Blommaert 1999, May 2004, 2012). In these conflicts, particular languages clearly *are* for many people an important and constitutive factor of their individual, and at times, collective identities. This is so, *even* when holding onto such languages has specific negative social and political consequences for their speakers, most often via active discrimination and/or oppression. As the sociolinguist, Adrian Blackledge, observes, 'We can hardly argue theoretically that for students who died protesting the right to establish Bengali as the national language of East Pakistan in 1952, language was not a key feature of identity' (2008, p. 33).[4] The *will* to maintain historically associated languages in often highly oppressive contexts problematizes, in turn, the notion of 'linguistic rational choice'. The assertion that speakers make decisions only on purely instrumentalist grounds, or at least that instrumental reasons are the only valid or rational choices available to minority language speakers, is at best one-sided, and at worst, simply wrong.

In theory then, language may well be just one of many markers of identity. In practice, it is often much more than that. In fact, this should not surprise us since the link between language and identity encompasses both significant cultural and political dimensions. The cultural dimension is demonstrated by the fact that one's individual and social identities, and their complex interconnections, are inevitably mediated in and through particular languages. The political dimension is significant to the extent that those languages come to be formally (and informally) associated with particular ethnic and national identities – something Van Parijs concedes, at least at the national level, in his subsequent advocacy of linguistic territoriality. These interconnections also help to explain why, as prominent sociolinguist Joshua Fishman (1997) argues, a 'detached' scientific view of the link between language and identity may fail to capture the degree to which language is *experienced* as vital by those who speak it.

Taking this more evenhanded approach (something with which Van Parijs is ostensibly centrally concerned; cf. Carens 2000) helps us to reconnect the instrumental and identity aspects of language. This is important because majority national languages, and international languages such as English even more so, are regularly dichotomized with minority languages on an instrumental-identity basis; majority languages fulfill the former function, minority languages the latter, or so the story goes (as we will see in the next section on diglossia). But this is simply not the case, since it is clear that *all* language(s) embody and accomplish both identity and instrumental functions for those who speak them (Joseph 2004, May 2012, Ch. 4). Where particular languages – especially majority/minority languages – differ is in the *degree* to which they can accomplish each of these functions, and this in turn is dependent on the social and political (not linguistic) constraints in which they operate (Carens 2000, May 2003, 2005). On this basis, the limited instrumentality of particular minority languages at any given time *need not always remain so*. Indeed, if the minority position of a language is the specific product of wider, often highly unequal, historical, and contemporary social and political relationships, changing these wider relationships positively with respect to a minority language should bring about both enhanced instrumentality for the language in question and increased mobility for its speakers. This is particularly so when that language is recognized in the public or civic realm.

The problem with diglossia

The attempt from a linguistic cosmopolitan perspective to turn language – specifically, the English language – into a mere (communicative) commodity, a neutral language in effect, is further undermined when we turn to Van Parijs's proposed solution to English as a global lingua franca for multilingual speakers – diglossia. Diglossia is where multilingual speakers continue to use their L1 and/or other local languages in local (read: low status) contexts, but English for wider (high-status) purposes, including, of course, those central to the processes of globalization (see also de Swaan 2001, Graddol 2007). Its promotion as an overt form of language policy can be traced back to the 1960s and 1970s, when early language planners adopted a similarly instrumentalist approach to issues of language in newly emergent postcolonial states in Africa, Asia, and the Middle East (for a useful overview, see Ricento 2006). The principal aim was to establish stable diglossic language contexts in which majority languages (usually, ex-colonial languages, and most often English and French) were promoted as public languages of wider communication. If promoted at all, local languages – minority languages, in effect – were seen as being limited to private, familial language domains. While concern was often expressed for the ongoing maintenance of local or minority languages, the principal emphasis of language policy at this time was on the establishment and promotion of 'unifying' national languages in postcolonial contexts, along the lines of their western, developed counterparts.

It is not hard to see how these broad precepts continue to underpin arguments for an expanded form of diglossia that now includes English as a global lingua franca – an approach that also reflects the asymmetric bilingualism with which Van Parijs is most familiar, both personally and professionally. But, as with early language planning efforts, such a position fails to address the fundamental status imbalances between local and so-called languages of wider communication in such contexts when they are constructed solely in terms of utility value. After all, if majority languages are consistently constructed as languages of 'wider communication' while minority languages are viewed as (merely) carriers of 'tradition' or 'historical identity', it is not hard to see what might become of the latter. Local(ized) or 'minority' languages will inevitably come to be viewed as delimited, perhaps even actively unhelpful languages – not only by others, but also often by their own speakers. This helps to explain the rapid expansion of language shift and loss from minority languages to majority languages – and, particularly, English – in the world today. Viewed in this light, the notion of 'stable diglossia' is itself a convenient fiction. Stable diglossia presupposes a degree of mutuality and reciprocity, along with a certain demarcation and boundedness between the majority and minority languages involved, when neither of these apply in real-world multilingual contexts. Situations of so-called stable diglossia are precisely *not* complementary in these respects. Rather, the normative ascendancy of dominant languages – and, particularly, English – specifically *militates* against the ongoing use, and even *existence* over time, of local languages. As Dua observes of the influence of English in India, for example,

> the complementarity of English with indigenous languages tends to go up in favour of English, partly because it is dynamic and cumulative in nature and scope, partly because it is sustained by socio-economic and market forces and partly because the educational system reproduces and legitimatizes the relations of power and knowledge implicated with English. (1994, p. 132)

Linguistic territoriality: a European 'solution'?

Similar tensions and contradictions exist in Van Parijs's advocacy of linguistic territoriality, which he views as a (or, rather, *the*) key bulwark against the very real potential for an unfettered English to usurp all other languages via the maxi-min principle. For Van Parijs, a 'territorially differentiated coercive linguistic regime' (2011, p. 136) is the only means of ensuring linguistic parity of esteem by which 'linguistic communities [can] preserve the societal culture associated with their language and thereby [protect] crucial resources required for leading an autonomous or meaningful life' (2011, p. 146). Echoing Kymlicka (1995, 2001), this would appear to acknowledge the symbolic significance of languages as a sufficient basis for their preservation, something which his advocacy of the maxi-min principle otherwise militates against. Thus, a given nation-state, or region, can maintain the public use of its historically associated languages via active institutional support – most often, in its required use in public education. Ostensibly, this position also allows for public multilingualism, *à l'européenne*. Indeed, Van Parijs is at pains to argue that linguistic territoriality differs substantively from the linguistic homogeneity of the traditional nation-state model (2011, p. 154ff.). On this basis, language rights, and associated institutional support can, for example, also be extended to regional majority languages in multinational federations, such as Catalan, Basque, or Welsh.

This is all well and good and is certainly a significant advance on the untrammeled public monolingualism of Anglo-American political theorists. But it is also little different from the European linguistic status quo where these kinds of 'promotion-oriented language rights' (May 2011)[5] are extended to only a small number of significant national minority groups, usually when they also comprise a regional majority (and, almost always, only after significant political advocacy/contest on behalf of the national minorities in question). All other linguistic minorities – including other national minority groups – fare far less well, since their languages remain consigned, largely, to diglossic, low-status, private language domains. In Europe, one only has to think of the differences between Catalan, Basque, and Welsh, on the one hand, and, say, Occitan, Breton, and Frisian, on the other. In short, the majority of Europe's national minority languages remain largely excluded from the public realm – the product of the visceral, state-sanctioned, linguistic nationalism of the last few centuries (Wright 2000, May 2012, see also Bauman and Briggs 2003). Not surprisingly, these European minority languages continue to decline rapidly in both status and number of speakers as a result, as numerous recent reviews make clear (see, e.g. Nelde *et al.* 1996, Extra and Gorter 2001, 2008).

And then, of course, there are immigrant languages, which do not generally receive any institutional support in Europe (or elsewhere). This skepticism toward immigrant languages is also clearly apparent in Van Parijs's (2011, p. 138) outright rejection of 'accommodative' language regimes, which might allow for such recognition. While I am not for a moment suggesting a carte blanche language rights approach to immigrant languages, there are nonetheless strong traditions in international law and within sociolinguistics that allow for the public recognition of immigrant languages in certain contexts and 'where numbers warrant' (May 2010, 2011). For example, there is growing agreement within international law that significant ethnic/immigrant minorities within a nation-state have a *reasonable* expectation to some form of state support (Carens 2000). In other words, while it would be unreasonable for nation-states to be required to fund language and education services for all minorities, it is increasingly accepted that, where a language is spoken by a significant number within the nation-state, it would also be unreasonable not to provide some level of state services and activity in that language (see May 2012, Ch. 5, for extended discussion). Such provisions also reinforce a *dynamic* cultural and linguistic conception of citizenship rather than the cultural and linguistic status quo ante that underpins Van Parijs's conception of linguistic territoriality.

The variability of English(es)

But let me return, in closing, to Van Parijs's central thesis – that English as global lingua franca provides not only the best means of cross-cultural communicative exchange in a globalized world, but also, crucially, upward social, economic, and educational mobility for other language speakers, irrespective of their first language(s). This voluntarist view of English language acquisition is flawed on two counts. First, as already suggested, it fails to address the wider economic, political, and ideological forces that shape and constrain such a choice at both the individual and the collective levels. Indeed, those, like Van Parijs, who advocate the 'benefits' of English largely fail to address the relationship between English and wider inequitable distributions and flows of wealth, resources, culture, and knowledge – especially in an increasingly globalized world. One obvious example of this can be found in the strong evidence that suggests that the adoption of English as an official language by nation-states has little influence on subsequent economic development. The poorest countries in Africa are for the most part those that have chosen English (or French) as an official language. Meanwhile, the majority of the Asian 'tiger economies' have opted instead for a local language, albeit usually in conjunction with English. In short, there is no necessary correlation between the adoption of English and greater economic well-being (Macedo *et al.* 2003). As Pennycook (1994, 1998) concludes, other factors, particularly the relative powerlessness and disadvantage experienced by such states within the wider nation-state system, exert far greater long-term influence.

Second, this position invariably presupposes that we all know what we actually mean when we talk about 'English', as if it is a monolithic category, equally available to all. And yet, in the real world of globalized late capitalism, fissured by disparities in developed and developing contexts, wealth, power, and inequality, neither is the case. Rather, English, as with any language, is in fact a complex agglomeration of many different varieties, used for widely varied purposes, in different contexts, and with widely different control, reach, and status. Echoing Dua's earlier observation on the links between social and economic forces, education, and the production of knowledge, it is in fact only *high-status* forms of English, along with high-level literacy skills, that can (possibly) accomplish significant upward mobility for their speakers. Not surprisingly, such high-prestige forms of English are predominantly the preserve of *existing* social and educational elites.[6] This elite/class-based access to high-prestige English language varieties complicates considerably the asserted links between English as a global lingua franca and upward social, economic, and educational mobility. Indeed, this basic assumption, demonstrably evident throughout Van Parijs's work, reflects a fundamental *naïveté* about the relationship between language varieties and access to power and opportunity. Van Parijs asserts that '[English] enables not only the rich and the powerful, but also the poor and the powerless to communicate, debate, network, cooperate, lobby and demonstrate effectively across borders' (2011, p. 31). On whose terms, one might ask, and to what ends (and with what reach/effect, given that many cannot reach across borders in the first instance)?[7] Contra these naïve and unsupported assertions, inequalities clearly continue to impact on those in developing contexts who actually speak particular, localized varieties of English, such as Indian English and Malay English, not only within these multilingual contexts themselves – on the basis of status and social class, for example (see also below) – but also between these contexts globally (Kachru 2004, Blommaert 2010).

In short, while those who learn these 'world Englishes' on a probability-driven basis (à la Van Parijs) might thus invest in them great hope for enhanced purchase and mobility, they are still most often judged pejoratively in relation to (more) prestigious English language varieties spoken by native speakers elsewhere. After all, the English acquired by urban Africans may offer them considerable purchase and prestige for their middle-class identities in African towns, but the same English may well be treated quite differently if they moved to London, identifying them as stigmatized, migrants, and from a lower class. The sociolinguist Jan Blommaert (2006, 2010) describes the latter as context-specific, 'low-mobility' forms of English (2010, p. 195). Context (and use) in relation to language varieties is thus, everything. As Blommaert (2006, p. 561) concludes,

> What is globalized is not an abstract Language, but specific speech forms, genres, styles, forms of literacy practice. And the way in which such globalized varieties enter into local environments is by a reordering [of] the locally available repertoires and the relative hierarchical relations between ingredients in the hierarchy.

The ongoing differential status still ascribed to these language varieties significantly undermines the related cosmopolitan presumption, also exemplified in Van Parijs's work, that multilingual speakers who speak English may be the new power brokers in a globalized world (see also Graddol 2007). As I have already argued, however, diglossia simply entrenches, rather than subverts, existing language hierarchies. As a result, we need to attend much more closely than Van Parijs's normative political philosophy allows to the specific *ethnographic* dimensions of (multiple) language use in particular contexts and what Anthony Liddicoat (2013) describes as the 'linguistic hierarchies of prestige' attendant upon them. In many postcolonial countries, for example, small English-speaking elites have deliberately continued the same policies as their former colonizers in order to ensure that (limited) access to English language education acts as a crucial distributor of social prestige and wealth (Heugh 2008, Ives 2010). Pattanayak (1969, 1985, 1990) and Dasgupta (1993) describe exactly this pattern in relation to India where English remained the preserve of a small, high-caste elite until at least the 1990s. The impact of globalization has changed this somewhat since then, particularly with the increasing use by multinational companies of business process outsourcing and information technology outsourcing requiring English language expertise (Graddol 2007). Examples here include call centers and publishing, both of which India has benefited directly from in the last decade. However, these developments also highlight the significant differentials and inequalities in pay and conditions for workers in India and other comparable contexts when compared with 'source' countries – indeed, these conditions are the principal *raison d'être* for the outsourcing in the first place. And, of course, the necessary English language expertise is still closely related to existing social class and related educational hierarchies in India, as elsewhere (Morgan and Ramanathan 2009, Sonntag 2009).

A similar scenario is evident in Africa where, despite English being an official or co-official language in as many as 15 postcolonial African states, the actual percentage of English speakers in each of these states never exceeds 20% (Ngũgĩ 1993, Heugh 2008). Alexandre (1972) has gone as far as to suggest that, in postcolonial Africa social class can be distinguished more clearly on linguistic than economic lines. While this observation willfully understates the coterminous nature of linguistic and social class stratification – in Africa, as elsewhere – it does usefully underscore how these class/linguistic distinctions can extend to the widely varied *types* of English language varieties also used in these contexts. This returns us to Blommaert's (2010) notion of 'low-mobility' forms of English vs. more high-mobility forms. In short, it is *existing* elites who benefit most from English – or, more accurately, those prestigious varieties of English to which they have preferential access (high-status, high-mobility varieties with normative accents and standardized orthographies). For the majority of other linguistic minority speakers, the wider structural disadvantages they consistently face, including poverty and delimited education,[8] along with the predominantly lower-mobility forms of English to which they have access, limit, even foreclose, any beneficial effects (Blommaert *et al.* 2006). Acquiring English is thus more often a palliative than a cure, masking rather than redressing deeper structural inequalities. As Peter Ives concludes of this,

Learning English, or any dominant language, is not inherently detrimental in the abstract, but the context in which it occurs often means that it helps to reinforce psychological, social and cultural fragmentation. Thus a 'global language' like English can never fulfill the role cosmopolitanism sets for it, that of helping those marginalized and oppressed by 'globalization' to be heard. (2010, p. 530)

Conclusion

And this brings me to my final considerations. It is demonstrably clear that *Linguistic Justice* is an important, sophisticated, and useful *contribution* to questions of language, inclusion, and mobility, particularly in a globalized world dominated by English. But, equally clearly, it is not an adequate, or even a particularly useful, *answer* to these questions. It fails to convince either on the merits of English as a global lingua franca or on the possibilities of maintaining linguistic parity of esteem for other language speakers. The notion of access to English enhancing social, economic, and educational mobility in a globalized world founders on its woefully poor understanding of the complexities of actual English language varieties and use, along with a fatal unwillingness to address the social, class, and contextual locatedness of high-prestige English language varieties. This in turn is a product of its unreflexive attempt to impose the elite multilingual European experience on the rest of the world. Meanwhile, linguistic parity of esteem in this formulation is simply not an option for the poorest and/or least powerful. Subject to the unregulated vicissitudes of the maxi-min principle, they would have likely lost their languages long before any coercive territorial regime could come charging to the rescue (although, of course, the latter would only apply to national and/or regional majority languages anyway). All this, coupled with its fundamentally reductive understanding of language, is why Van Parijs's liberal egalitarian account of linguistic justice, for all its admirable intentions, can never accomplish the wider redistributive goals to which it (rightly) aspires. Indeed, the solutions offered by Van Parijs's account are much more likely to entrench linguistic (and related social and political) inequalities than ameliorate them.

Disclosure statement

No potential conflict of interest was reported by the author.

Notes

1. As I have argued elsewhere (May 2003, 2014b), such a serious and sustained treatment of language as a topic in its own right remains rare within political philosophy – not least, because the ongoing dominance of liberal accounts of justice therein militates against acknowledgment of the significance of language to individual and group identity in the first instance and, thus, any associated rights claims.

2. This is not particular to Van Parijs's account but is reflective of a more generalized unwillingness by political theorists who address language to engage in relevant sociolinguistic literature. I have made this point previously in relation to both opponents of language rights, such as Pogge, and Laitin and Reich (May 2003), as well as proponents such as Kymlicka (May 2012, Ch. 4). For a similar critique, see Ives (2006, 2010).

3. As we shall see, Van Parijs does acknowledge symbolic considerations of language when they are associated with national and regional majority languages – a mitigating argument he outlines in his advocacy for linguistic territoriality.

4. Contra to Van Parijs's assertion (2011, p. 153), following Laitin (2004), that the institutionalization of language rights increases ethnic conflict, any diachronic, contextualized view of ethnic conflicts reveals that it is the *denial* of language rights, not their recognition, which is often a motive force in ethnic conflict. Along with Bengali vs. Urdu in East Pakistan/Bangladeshi, these include, to name but a few, Catalan and Basque in Franco's Spain; Sinhalese vs. Tamil in Sri Lanka; Albanian vs. Serbian in Kosovo; Tibetan vs. Chinese in Chinese-controlled Tibet, as well as of course Flemish vs. French in Van Parijs' Belgium.

5. Promotion-oriented rights, a term first developed by the sociolinguist Heinz Kloss (1971, 1977), regulate the extent to which minority language rights are recognized within the public domain, including in key public institutions such as schools. Promotion-oriented language rights can thus include, for example, state-funded education in a minority language, along the lines that Van Parijs is arguing.

6. Van Parijs unwittingly reinforces this point in his preoccupation with the spread of English across Europe. For example, the Eurobarometer (2006), upon which he draws for his supporting empirical basis, consistently highlights that those most likely to acquire English as an additional language are young, well-educated professionals and/or from European countries with the greatest social wealth and political influence (see also Lacey 2013).

7. I am reminded here of the sociologist Craig Calhoun's (2007) critique of cosmopolitanism more generally, which he argues consistently ignores the class-based, privileged, nature of so-called cosmopolitans – the 'frequent flyers' of the contemporary world. As he acerbically observes, advocacy of cosmopolitan identities within social and political theory 'obscures the issues of inequality that make [such] identities accessible mainly to elites and make being a comfortable citizen of the world contingent on having the right passports, credit cards, and cultural credentials' (2007, p. 286). By framing cosmopolitanism appeals to humanity in individualistic terms, he continues, 'they are apt to privilege those with the most capacity to get what they want by individual action' (2007, p. 295).

8. This includes, crucially, English-medium education, often implemented in many developing contexts precisely on the basis of the misconceived views of English outlined here. Taught poorly by teachers who themselves may not have sufficient English language skills (or relevant teaching expertise), such education simply entrenches educational disadvantage rather than ameliorating it – not least, because it ignores the best means of achieving educational success, being taught in one's L1 in the first instance (see May 2014a for further discussion).

Notes on contributors

Stephen May is Professor of Education in Te Puna Wananga (School of Maori Education) in the Faculty of Education, The University of Auckland, New Zealand, and a leading international authority on language rights, language policy, and language education. To date, he has published 14 books and over 90 academic articles and book chapters in these areas. His key books include *Language and Minority Rights* (2nd edition; Routledge, 2012), the 1st edition of which received an American Library Association Choice's Outstanding Academic title award (2008). His latest book is a significant new edited collection, *The Multilingual Turn* (Routledge, 2014). He has previously edited, with Nancy Hornberger, *Language Policy and Political Issues in Education,* Volume 1 of the *Encyclopedia of Language and Education* (2nd edition.; Springer, 2008) and with Christine Sleeter, *Critical Multiculturalism: Theory and Praxis* (Routledge, 2010). He is General Editor of the 3rd edition of the 10-volume *Encyclopedia of Language and Education* (Springer, 2016), a Founding Editor of the interdisciplinary journal, *Ethnicities* (Sage), and Associate Editor of *Language Policy* (Springer). His homepage is http://www.education.auckland.ac.nz/uoa/stephen-may.

References

Alexandre, P., 1972. *Languages and language in Black Africa.* Evanston, IL: Northwestern University Press.

Archibugi, D., 2005. The language of democracy: vernacular or esperanto? A comparison between the multiculturalist and cosmopolitan perspectives. *Political studies,* 53 (3), 537–555.

Banton, M., 1987. *Racial theories.* Cambridge: Cambridge University Press.

Barry, B., 2001. *Culture and equality: an egalitarian critique of multiculturalism.* Cambridge, MA: Harvard University Press.

Barth, F., 1969. *Ethnic groups and boundaries: the social organization of culture difference.* Boston, MA: Little, Brown.

Bauman, R. and Briggs, C., 2003. *Voices of modernity.* Cambridge: Cambridge University Press.

Bishop, R. and Phillips, J., 2006. Language. *Theory, culture & society,* 23 (2–3), 51–69.

Blackledge, A., 2008. Language ecology and language ideology. *In*: A. Creese, P. Martin, and N. Hornberger, eds. *Ecology of language. Encyclopedia of language and education,* 2nd ed., vol. 9. New York: Springer, 27–40.

Blommaert, J., ed., 1999. *Language ideological debates.* Berlin: Mouton de Gruyter.

Blommaert, J., 2006. A sociolinguistics of globalization. *In*: N. Coupland and A. Jaworski, eds. *The new sociolinguistics reader.* Basingstoke: Palgrave Macmillan, 560–573.

Blommaert, J., 2010. *The sociolinguistics of globalization.* New York: Cambridge University Press.

Blommaert, J., *et al.*, 2006. Peripheral normativity: literacy and the production of locality in a South African township school. *Linguistics and education,* 16, 378–403.

Brutt-Griffler, J., 2002. Class, ethnicity, and language rights: an analysis of British colonial policy in Lesotho and Sri Lanka and some implications for language policy. *Journal of language, identity and education,* 1 (3), 207–234.

Calhoun, C., 2007. Social solidarity as a problem for cosmopolitan democracy. *In*: S. Benhabib, I. Shapiro, and D. Petranovich, eds. *Identities, affiliations, and allegiances.* Cambridge: Cambridge University Press, 285–302.

Carens, J., 2000. *Culture, citizenship, and community.* Oxford: Oxford University Press.

Dasgupta, P., 1993. *The otherness of English: India's auntie tongue syndrome.* London: Sage.

De Swaan, A., 2001. *Words of the world: The global language system.* Cambridge: Polity Press.

Dua, H., 1994. *Hegemony of English.* Mysore: Yashoda.

Edwards, J., 1994. *Multilingualism.* London: Routledge.

Edwards, J., 2009. *Language and identity.* Cambridge: Cambridge University Press.

Edwards, J., 2010. *Minority languages and group identity: cases and categories*. Amsterdam: John Benjamins.

Eurobarometer. 2006. *Europeans and their languages*. Eurobarometer 64, 3. Luxembourg: European Commission.

Extra, G. and Gorter, D., eds., 2001. *The other languages of Europe: demographic, sociolinguistic and educational perspectives*. Clevedon: Multilingual Matters.

Extra, G. and Gorter, D., eds., 2008. *Multilingual Europe: facts and policies*. Berlin: Mouton de Gruyter.

Fishman, J., 1997. Language and ethnicity: the view from within. *In*: F. Coulmas, ed. *The handbook of sociolinguistics*. Oxford: Blackwell, 327–343.

Graddol, D., 2007. *English next: why global English may mean the end of 'English as a foreign language'*. London: British Council.

Hechter, M., 1986. Rational choice theory and the study of race and ethnic relations. *In*: J. Rex and D. Mason, eds. *Theories of race and ethnic relations*. Cambridge: Cambridge University Press, 264–279.

Heugh, K., 2008. Language policy in Southern Africa. *In*: S. May and N. Hornberger, eds. *Encyclopedia of language and education. Language policy and political issues in education*, 2nd ed., vol. 1, New York: Springer, 355–367.

Ives, P., 2006. 'Global English': linguistic imperialism or practical lingua franca? *Studies in language & capitalism*, 1, 121–141. Available from: http://citeseerx.ist.psu. edu/viewdoc/download?doi=10.1.1.118.4193&rep=rep1&type=pdf#page=124.

Ives, P., 2010. Cosmopolitanism and global English: language politics in globalisation debates. *Political studies*, 58 (3), 516–535.

Joseph, J., 2004. *Language and identity*. Basingstoke: Palgrave Macmillan.

Kachru, B., 2004. *Asian Englishes: beyond the canon*. Hong Kong: Hong Kong University Press.

Kloss, H., 1971. Language rights of immigrant groups. *International migration review*, 5, 250–268.

Kloss, H., 1977. *The American bilingual tradition*. Rowley, MA: Newbury House.

Kymlicka, W., 1995. *Multicultural citizenship: a liberal theory of minority rights*. Oxford: Clarendon Press.

Kymlicka, W., 2001. *Politics in the vernacular*. Oxford: Oxford University Press.

Lacey, J., 2013. Considerations on English as a global lingua franca. *Political studies review*, doi:10.1111/1478-9302.12004.

Laitin, D., 2004. Language policy and civil war. *In*: P. Van Parijs, ed. *Cultural diversity versus economic solidarity*. Brussels: De Boeck, 171–188.

Laitin, D. and Reich, R., 2003. A liberal democratic approach to language justice. *In*: W. Kymlicka and A. Patten, eds. *Language rights and political theory*. Oxford: Oxford University Press, 80–104.

Liddicoat, A., 2013. *Language-in-education policies: the discursive construction of intercultural relations*. Bristol: Multilingual Matters.

Macedo, D., Dendrinos, B., and Gounari, P., 2003. *The hegemony of English*. Boulder, CO: Paradigm.

May, S., 2003. Misconceiving minority language rights: implications for liberal political theory. *In*: W. Kymlicka and A. Patten, eds. *Language rights and political theory*. Oxford: Oxford University Press, 123–152.

May, S., 2004. Rethinking linguistic human rights: answering questions of identity, essentialism and mobility. *In*: D. Patrick and J. Freeland, eds. *Language rights and language 'survival': a sociolinguistic exploration*. Manchester: St Jerome, 35–53.

May, S., 2005. Language rights: moving the debate forward. *Journal of sociolinguistics*, 9 (3), 319–347.

May, S., 2010. Derechos lingüísticos como derechos humanos [Linguistic rights as human rights]. *Revista de Antropología Social*, 19, 131–159.

May, S., 2011. Language rights: the "Cinderella" human right. *Journal of human rights*, 10 (3), 265–289.

May, S., 2012. *Language and minority rights: ethnicity, nationalism and the politics of language*. 2nd ed. New York: Routledge.

May, S., 2014a. Justifying educational language rights. *Review of research in education (RRE) [Language diversity and language policy and politics in education]*, 38 (1), 215–241.

May, S., 2014b. Contesting public monolingualism and diglossia: rethinking political theory and language policy for a multilingual world. *Language policy*, 13 (4), 371–393.

May, S., Modood, T., and Squires, J., 2004. Ethnicity, nationalism and minority rights: charting the disciplinary debates. *In*: S. May, T. Modood, and J. Squires, eds. *Ethnicity, nationalism, and minority rights*. Cambridge: Cambridge University Press, 1–24.

Morgan, B. and Ramanathan, V., 2009. Outsourcing, globalizing economics, and shifting language policies: issues in managing Indian call centres. *Language policy*, 8 (1), 69–80.

Nelde, P., Strubell, M., and Williams, G., 1996. *Euromosaic: the production and reproduction of the minority language groups in the European Union*. Luxembourg: Office for Official Publications of the European Communities.

Pattanayak, D., 1969. *Aspects of applied linguistics*. London: Asia Publishing House.

Pattanayak, D., 1985. Diversity in communication and languages; predicament of a multilingual nation state: India, a case study. *In*: N. Wolfson and J. Manes, eds. *Language of inequality*. Berlin: Mouton de Gruyter, 399–407.

Pattanayak, D., ed., 1990. *Multilingualism in India*. Clevedon: Multilingual Matters.

Pennycook, A., 1994. *The cultural politics of English as an international language*. London: Longman.

Pennycook, A., 1998. *English and the discourses of colonialism*. London: Routledge.

Pogge, T., 2003. Accommodation rights for Hispanics in the US. *In*: W. Kymlicka and A. Patten, eds. *Language rights and political theory*. Oxford: Oxford University Press, 105–122.

Ricento, T., ed., 2006. *An introduction to language policy*. New York: Blackwell.

Rubio-Marín, R., 2003. Language rights: exploring the competing rationales. *In*: W. Kymlicka and A. Patten, eds. *Language rights and political theory*. Oxford: Oxford University Press, 52–79.

Sonntag, S., 2009. Linguistic globalization and the call center industry: imperialism, hegemony or cosmopolitanism? *Language policy*, 8 (1), 5–25.

Ngũgĩ, wa Thiong'o, 1993. *Moving the centre: the struggle for cultural freedoms*. London: James Currey.

Van Parijs, P., 2004. Europe's linguistic challenge. *European journal of sociology*, 45 (1), 113–154.

Van Parijs, P., 2011. *Linguistic justice for Europe and for the world*. Oxford: Oxford University Press.

Weinstein, B., 1983. *The civic tongue: political consequences of language choices*. New York: Longman.

Wright, S., 2000. *Community and communication: the role of language in nation state building and European integration*. Clevedon: Multilingual Matters.

Lingua franca fever: sceptical remarks

Denise Réaume[a,b]

[a]Faculty of Law, University of Toronto, Toronto, ON, Canada; [b]Faculty of Law, University of Oxford, Oxford, UK

The policy push in favour of fostering a global *lingua franca* has shed overtly imperialistic underpinnings and been recast, but many of the same objections can be levelled at new attempts to justify an old policy. Efforts to explain the impetus towards linguistic uniformity through rational choice theory obscure the power dynamics behind choice of language in multilingual contexts. Invoking democratic engagement as a benefit of uniformity overestimates the role of linguistic diversity as a drag on participation and ignores more important forces. A focus on equality of opportunity and social mobility through *lingua franca* competence as justification for the policy reveals a shallow conception of equality and underplays the long-term consequences for non-*lingua franca* communities were equality of opportunity for individuals to be taken seriously. Finally, seeing the justice issues that arise out of competition between languages as one of ensuring adequate compensation to the losers underscores how thin is the conception of equality animating the approach; it purchases an inadequate level of equal opportunity for individuals at the expense of inequality amongst language communities.

Language policy: three models

Three basic models guide language policy.[1] At opposite poles, the integration (sometimes called harmonisation, or assimilation) model advocates adoption/ promotion of a single language, while the maintenance (sometimes called nationalist, or survival) model tends to the view that (all) languages should be preserved. In between, the multilingualism (or equal recognition) model holds that some public recognition and support should be provided for languages when they interact, but rejects the idea that survival of each language is of paramount importance. I favour this last view (Réaume 1991, 1995).

Advocates of the integration model also tend to see the emergence of one *lingua franca* as inevitable. For some, inevitability is justification enough – what must be, must be good. But some have taken on the challenge of articulating what is desirable about the existence of a *lingua franca*. The defenders of linguistic pluralism in either guise tend to reject the inevitability thesis and focus on the injustice of the pressure placed on other languages and their speakers by the dominance of the *lingua franca*.

An important contributor to this debate is Van Parijs (2003, 2007, 2011) who seeks to shake up these settled positions by arguing both that the emergence of English as a *lingua franca* (in Europe and globally) is both inevitable and desirable *and* that it is unfair. Drawing on rational choice theory to demonstrate the inevitability thesis, he then calls in aid the values of democracy, social mobility and social justice to justify hastening the process. However, he argues that the unfairness arising from integration calls for compensation and mitigation, providing the best of both worlds – the benefits of a *lingua franca* and justice for other language speakers. Recognising that linguistic integration comes at a cost is unusual amongst those with *lingua franca* fever; more common is the tendency to treat pluralists as silly romantics or linguistic tyrants. So Van Parijs bridges one theoretical divide that has characterised much of the debate. My remarks are nonetheless directed at raising doubts about his vision of a happy equilibrium.

Each layer of Van Parijs' theory is open to challenge. Rational choice theory obscures the power dynamics behind choice of language in multilingual contexts. Invoking democratic engagement overestimates the role of linguistic diversity as a drag on participation and ignores more important forces. Aiming to ensure equality of opportunity and social mobility through *lingua franca* competence reveals a shallow conception of equality and underplays the long-term consequences for non-*lingua franca* communities were equality of opportunity to be taken seriously. Finally, the forms of compensation recommended underscore how thin is the conception of equality animating the approach; it purchases an inadequate level of equal opportunity for individuals at the expense of inequality amongst language communities.

The inevitability of integration – underlying assumptions

Van Parijs (2011, p. 12) identifies two features of the decision context creating pressure towards the emergence of a *lingua franca*. The first of these forces is the probability-sensitive nature of language learning: it is rational to choose to learn the second language that one has reason to believe is most likely to be useable. This situates the issue in the context of a mainly instrumental understanding of the point of language use based on the communicative function of language. I prefer to label this aspect of language use as information transfer rather than communication, for reasons that should become clear.

It would be foolish to deny that language is an instrument that can serve ends independent of it. If I want to sell widgets or work in the service sector, and the buyers or customers speak language A, using A will serve my ends better than using any other language, however much I may be attached to another. But notice that the same is true for A-speakers wishing to deal with non-A-speakers – if the likelihood of interaction and the usefulness of effective communication were sufficiently great, it would be rational for A-speakers wishing to communicate with non-A-speakers to learn *their* language(s). The forces are symmetrical unless we introduce other factors. By itself, probability sensitivity does not dictate linguistic integration. Of course, if there are 100 times more A-speakers than B-speakers, and B-speakers are as likely to want to sell widgets to A-speakers as to members of their own language group, their learning to speak A is much more useful for a B-speaker than *vice versa*. But such a simple model cannot explain the inevitability of *English* as the *lingua franca* – certainly not in Europe; not even globally.

The elephant in the room is that the current usefulness of English stems from the economic, political and cultural power of, first, the British Empire, and more lately the American Empire. The use of that power has been bound up with the use and promotion of English. Political/military power paved the way for cultural dominance, now consolidated under market forces substantially controlled by multinational corporations run in English. Thus, it is misleading to treat the usefulness of English as a *mere* fact, and its rise as a benign result of a 'haphazard sequence of events' (Van Parijs 2011, p. 22). Van Parijs acknowledges that power plays some role in this history, but minimises the obvious injustices involved in its exercise. For example, English did not simply 'slowly spread' across Britain (Van Parijs 2011, p. 22); its introduction into Wales was fostered by the legal repression of Welsh (Law in Wales Act, 1535); its dominance in Scotland was supported by the Highland clearances. Van Parijs' passing reference (2011, p. 22) to the 'help of gunpowder and lethal bugs' in explaining the toehold English gained in the New World belittles the deliberate devastation inflicted on Aboriginal peoples and their cultures. Nor did English happen to be the first European language to establish itself in North America, so that 'it was therefore into English, rather than into German, Italian, or Spanish that linguistic assimilation proceeded' (Van Parijs 2011, p. 23). On the contrary, German was actively repressed in colonial Pennsylvania, French in Louisiana, and Spanish throughout the southwestern United States (Piatt 1993, Crawford 2000), paving the way for engineering waves of migration by English speakers in a planned effort to inundate other languages.[2]

This ugly history matters. The impetus towards second language learning may seem now to be taking place under more benign market-like conditions of equality between different language communities, but pre-existing inequalities are an important part of what makes a particular language salient in the complex coordination problem of translingual conversation.

The second dynamic pushing towards convergence on a *lingua franca* is the 'maxi-min communication' strategy: in a multilingual group, it is rational to choose the language of which the most people have at least some understanding (Van Parijs 2011, p. 13). Again, this draws its power from the information transfer context. Some understanding of a language, however modest, is better than nothing if one needs to convey basic information. Now, basic information can be quite important: say, informing people about a fire in the building or the car crash up ahead. However, this describes only a very narrow range of ways in which, or reasons for which, language is used.

The maxi-min strategy is sensible for simple transactions in the market square, but not for understanding a poem, conducting diplomatic negotiations or making a subtle point in court. In these contexts, nothing but a high level of language competence will do, so a speaker will want to speak the language she speaks best. Those unable to follow along will be left out, or if the speaker's language is one that few share, she will be effectively silenced. That is, unless alternative strategies to facilitate communication are possible. Yet resorting to a language that most participants, perhaps including the speaker, speak only minimally well is a non-starter in some contexts, not the best we can do under challenging circumstances. Struggling to write a poem in a language not fully mastered so that everyone may know it is about a tree misses the point of writing poetry in the first place or wanting others to enjoy it.

This, as we shall see, has implications for linguistic justice. The push for a *lingua franca* often comes from the market square, that is, simple transactions achievable with rough and basic communication. But if a *lingua franca* takes hold in that domain and we generalise the model, there are consequences for those on whom the burden of learning a new language is imposed. I return to these issues below.

Another assumption lies behind the maxi-min strategy, at least as part of an explanation of why *English* is emerging as the *lingua franca*. Why is English a better bet in Europe than German or French? Because anglophones are often part of the conversation, and the one sure thing is that most of them will speak only English. Monolingualism is less true of native speakers of other European languages. The more others adapt to anglophone incompetence or intransigence, the more the salience of English is entrenched.

Those willing to learn another language, even rudimentarily, will be at a disadvantage in the company of those who refuse to do so, at least if the willing learners have an interest in their language becoming the *lingua franca*. In principle, willingness to learn ought to be equally distributed amongst all peoples, but in practice willingness or lack thereof often stems from previously entrenched forms of social inequality. Anglophones do not just happen not to speak a second or third language; they largely exist in a social and political culture that has entitled them not to do so, and they often feel no obligation to meet others even half way.

Absent these forms of social power, and thus privilege, it is questionable whether a single *lingua franca* would emerge at all, let alone that it would be English. To the extent that Van Parijs acknowledges this dynamic in the parable of his tussle with his father-in-law over the hoovering (2011, pp. 51–52), he treats it as grounds for compensation for an unfair outcome rather than a reason to prevent unfair outcomes from emerging. If a particular state of affairs is inevitable, though unfair, we should just figure out how to go forward as fairly as possible. But if that situation might not exist if not for unjust power relations that brought it into being, it is less clear that the only task of a theory of linguistic justice is to determine how best to compensate for the way things turned out. This is especially so where the result has not yet quite emerged; in this context, the decision to treat it as inevitable will itself make its emergence a foregone conclusion. The remedy for the injustice of one household member doing all the hoovering is, *prima facie*, to take turns doing it, unless the person otherwise bearing the entire cost prefers some other form of redress.

Inevitability often serves to lighten the burden of making sound normative arguments in favour of the end advocated: if a phenomenon is inevitable, we may as well accentuate the positive. But there are reasons to doubt the force of the arguments in favour of a *lingua franca* world and arguments against are often underplayed.

The positive benefits of a *lingua franca* – some doubts

The arguments for welcoming and even fostering the emergence of a *lingua franca* have vastly increased in complexity in recent scholarship.[3] The dominant argument used to be straightforwardly efficiency-based. It would be so much easier and cheaper to get on with things if everyone all spoke the same language. Recent writing counts efficiency as a plus, but puts it well down the list of integration's benefits. Instead, the existence of a *lingua franca* is now said to be a necessary precondition of robust democratic engagement and a vibrant transnational civil society.[4] At the same time, some integrationists infuse the project with an egalitarian concern for social mobility and opportunity (Patten 2007, Van Parijs 2011, pp. 26–27). Van Parijs (2011, pp. 24–27) adds the further idea that a *lingua franca* will promote what he calls 'ethical contagion' – the ability and willingness of the globally advantaged to include the disadvantaged in their conception of global social justice. The strongest version of the argument melds all of these elements: genuine democracy requires that all members of society be able to participate, democracy and social life generally are enhanced by civil society groups of all sorts pursuing various interests, public and private, and the equal ability of all members of society to participate in governance and civil society and the market as well as our ability to embrace a global conception of social justice requires comprehensive access to a *lingua franca*. If the new arguments fail to bolster the case for integration, we may suspect that the driving force remains efficiency.

The egalitarian rationale for fostering a *lingua franca* not only individualises that project but treats it as a matter of distributive justice *for individuals*.[5] Pursuing comprehensive *lingua franca* competence exacerbates the conflict between the informational and the expressive use of language for non-*lingua franca*-speaking communities. That this conflict is frequently downplayed reveals a problem with a rational choice approach. An account of rational behaviour that illuminates the context of the market square produces results that might well be regarded as irrational in contexts more like an arts and letters society.

As we shall see, these egalitarian concerns push for ever-greater *lingua franca* penetration. While there has always been a need for different language communities to cooperate, traditionally this was achieved through a cadre of multilingual professionals who communicated their discussions to their respective linguistic constituencies. This model is now increasingly branded as elitist. The argument seems to be that unless all members of a multilingual community can speak directly to each other – in parliament, in NGO meetings, on radio and television and on the Internet, in the full array of contexts in which there are views, ideas and information to be communicated – we cannot have a genuine democracy or a vibrant civil society, nor do we foster 'ethical contagion'. There are two bases for scepticism here: first, it is unclear how effective a common language is at fostering engagement in a common debate or acceptance of an inclusive global politics; second, it is doubtful that a common language is necessary to produce an informed citizenry.

Does a common language foster democratic engagement and global solidarity?

It is too optimistic to attribute to a *lingua franca* the power to significantly advance the pursuit of meaningful democracy and social justice on a global scale, however worthy these aims. More unilingual societies are not more appreciably democratic or just than otherwise comparable plurilingual ones. Those who watch Fox News seldom tune into MSNBC, let alone Democracy Now!, and are indifferent to the plight of the disadvantaged in their midst, even though they have every opportunity to interact and even converse with them. It would be nice to think that political consensus and common commitment to global social justice would emerge from better understanding and more opportunities for communication, but if speaking a common language does not seem very effective at breaking down entrenched conflicting political interests in the domestic context, it is hard to see why we should place more faith in it at the global level.

Is a lingua franca necessary to a vibrant democracy?

Of course, some movement across the linguistic divide must occur to have a conversation about matters of mutual interest, but why must (almost) everyone be able to use a single language? Democracy does not require that every participant be able to communicate directly with every other participant. It is enough if a certain percentage in each group is bilingual or multilingual. How many varies with the range and complexity of the interaction between the different communities, and perhaps with the population ratio between groups. But a relatively small minority would do, concentrated in certain sectors and occupations – the media, policy-makers, perhaps all or part of the academy. Provided enough people in these sectors were capable of speaking other languages, it should be possible for the ideas and perspectives from other linguistic communities to be digested internally and disseminated to those without that second language competence. For informed debate to take place, everyone must have access to the lines of thought in the debate; it is not important that access be direct.[6]

Insisting on full linguistic integration in order to facilitate political debate is like assuming that each must understand climatology if we are to have a serious discussion about climate change. A healthy democracy and vibrant civil society can work with a significant division of labour. Language differences cannot be a greater obstacle to debate than other disparities in expertise. Arguably, lack of a common language is amongst the least important, and most easily remedied, sources of disagreement in our divided societies. Most people, for example, have only an imperfect understanding of what caused the recent economic crisis or what might fix it. The media present prescriptions of duelling economic and financial experts. It is difficult to figure out who is right. And yet, opinions are formed and ballots cast. At least adding voices from other language communities to the debate merely requires accurate reporting of what *their* duelling experts say, a task much easier for the multilingual class to handle than that of any of us in puzzling through the experts we can read directly.

In fact, none of the sectors in which multilingualism would be handy is presently doing a good job of providing this kind of filtering and translation service to the rest of society. The problem is particularly noticeable in the media. But it seems overkill to encourage *everyone* to learn a common language rather than promoting multiple language competence as an important qualification for employment in media organisations, the civil service and universities. If there are other sectors that should be added to the list, let's add them, but we should still be able to ensure communication by encouraging multilingualism in a fairly small population.

Not that it would be easy to change the culture of these sectors or to establish the kind of language training required. Indeed, media organisations have been shedding journalists rather than investing in their human capital (McChesney and Nicols 2010). But the obstacles to multilingualism in these key sectors have more to do with entrenched privilege or the profit imperative than concern for the ideal conditions for democratic debate.

The egalitarian twist: the tail wagging the dog

The charge of elitism aimed at the traditional method of securing cooperation stems from a concern that it fails to provide equal opportunity to join the multilingual cadre. Economically advantaged parents will ensure that their children get language training while less advantaged children will be frozen out of important opportunities. Comprehensive *lingua franca* competence is meant to better ensure equal opportunity. But this oversimplifies the sources of, and remedy for, inequality.

In every society, the well off enjoy advantages in respect of their prospects. The wealthy send their children to better schools, give them ballet or hockey lessons, introduce them to the right people. When a new way emerges to give their children a leg up – financially supporting a child so she can accept an unpaid internship, for example – wealthy parents will use it. So if one cannot become Prime Minister or the Editor of The Times unless one has more than one language, ambitious parents will ensure their children speak multiple languages. However, advocating universal *lingua franca* competence in response is a case of the tail wagging the dog.

First, the advantage parents might confer on their children through language training is marginal. If equal opportunity for all children were our main objective, we should improve publicly funded education systems and make university accessible, for example, rather than providing universal *lingua franca* training. Second, against a backdrop of pervasive inequality, giving everyone the opportunity to learn the *lingua franca* is not going to stop parents with means purchasing better education in the *lingua franca* for their children, ensuring greater fluency and a more standard accent.

Evening out the quality of *lingua franca* learning, if even possible, would take several generations (and substantial expenditure). In the meantime, a great many people will still be denied equal access to many opportunities. And, of course, even when we reach communicative nirvana, other forms of inequality will still dictate that some have significantly better life chances than others, and these have a much greater impact on average than linguistic competence disparities. The vast majority still lives and works close to home, linguistically speaking. Must we give everyone *lingua franca* competence for the sake of guaranteeing each a chance to be part of the smallish percentage of globetrotters? The percentage of people able to exploit professional opportunities in a global economy has increased, but it is an egalitarian pipe dream to imagine that whole populations could enjoy such opportunities in any realistic timeframe.

If we are going to forego having a common means of communication, we should of course attend to the consequences from the perspective of social equality. It is less clear that concern about those consequences argues in favour of linguistic integration. Most of the solutions proposed by Van Parijs to remedy the unfairness of asymmetry between language groups aim at greater penetration of the *lingua franca* and higher competence levels in second language speakers.[7] The egalitarian argument is a red herring that ultimately serves to obscure the real costs of fostering the emergence of a *lingua franca*.

The costs of a *lingua franca*

Van Parijs' advocacy of a *lingua franca* oversimplifies the range of uses and values that language has for its speakers and then fails to work out the implications of his rational choice model for the long-term viability of language communities. He is alert to the danger of language decline, but because he treats the emergence of a *lingua franca* as inevitable, he undervalues the loss it imposes. Further, he seems insouciant about how the pursuit of social equality through fostering the emergence of a *lingua franca* will exacerbate the conflict between participating in the *lingua franca* conversation and contributing to the vibrancy of one's native tongue.

The costs of the emergence of a *lingua franca* can be counted, first, in the time and effort involved for those who undertake to learn another language. Beyond that is the damage to the viability of one's own language, assuming widespread success in acquiring the *lingua franca*.

Van Parijs (2011, pp. 91–95) acknowledges that the native speakers of the language that becomes the *lingua franca* enjoy a substantial social advantage. But he paints this largely as a matter of the ease with which one can communicate, which is then paired with the effort required of non-native speakers to learn. This underplays the benefits to native speakers and consequently the costs of not being a native speaker, especially against the backdrop of the social equality discussed above.

The comprehensive pursuit of linguistic integration would involve use of the *lingua franca* in as many spheres of language use as possible, from the market square to the arts and letters club. Of course, at this level of ambition, this would not happen quickly, but if the goal is desirable, one might well advocate making a start. The more comprehensive we make the reach of the *lingua franca*, the greater the demands on the second language skills of non-native speakers. At the same time, the greater the advantage is for native speakers, at least for the foreseeable future.

Not only do native speakers have to exert less effort to get their point across in mixed settings, but the more the context requires sophisticated language skills, the more effective native speakers will be in controlling the discussion.[8] Anyone who has been to a conference conducted in English at which some papers are presented in English by inexpert non-native speakers knows that the latter tend to generate less discussion and make less of an impression. This dynamic extends also to less formal settings. Consider, for example, the sorts of civil society organisations in which Van Parijs is concerned to secure participation. Even in an Amnesty International meeting, we can expect the anglophones to dominate the conversation. And if the group seeks to influence governments and liaise with other organisations, it will be those with the best language skills who will rise to positions of authority. In a wide range of spheres in which different languages come together, non-native speakers of the *lingua franca* will be at a disadvantage in gaining power and influence. Over time, the relative power of English speakers will be consolidated and tend to become systemic. Van Parijs' own rational choice approach predicts this result: because universal *lingua franca* competence cannot be achieved immediately, the importance of getting the job at hand done will always trump considerations of fairness towards those whose language skills are not as strong.

There are two problems here. First, power, once amassed, tends to become entrenched. Those in power tend to choose their successors and can control an organisation's agenda, allowing them subtly to favour the interests of people like them, even if unconsciously. Since second language learning takes time, the advantage of anglophones will often become very firmly entrenched, making it an enormous struggle for others to achieve equal participation. Second, the only way non-native speakers can hope to overcome the built-in advantage held by native speakers is to perfect their competence in the *lingua franca*. The best way to compete for the attention of others against the best talent from the native *lingua franca* speakers is to speak the language as well as they do. This drives up the cost of second language learning enormously. We are no longer talking about giving everyone a copy of Berlitz, but rather transforming education systems in dramatic ways.

The modesty of the compensatory measures Van Parijs proposes shows that his model assumes roughly the context of the market square when evaluating the cost to second language learners, though he claims to be concerned about equal access to all realms of communication. Banning the use of dubbing in English language films (Van Parijs 2011, pp. 109–113) will help non-English speakers acquire the language, but its effect will surely be marginal. Hollywood blockbusters and sit-coms certainly would not prepare anyone to write a grant proposal, a brief to parliament or a land use planning body, or even an op-ed piece. Allowing non-English speakers to poach English language materials from the web (Van Parijs 2011, pp. 78–81) may aid in language acquisition, but that is still a long way from producing widespread high competence. These are cheap, but at best only modestly and very gradually effective, forms of 'compensation'. Most who bear the brunt of the initial transitional costs of second language learning will not share in the ultimate benefits of linguistic integration. Van Parijs' suggestions merely marginally reduce the costs imposed on them.

Nothing but first-class second language education could level the playing field. Although Van Parijs (2011) thinks compensation for the costs of language learning is due, he is not naïve enough to expect money to change hands – hence the forms of in-kind compensation he proposes. He is surely right that anglophone countries will not underwrite the actual cost of proper language learning, but this leaves the equality concern unmet. In the absence of good quality, publicly funded *lingua franca* training available to all, the already advantaged will continue to ensure the advantage of linguistic competence for their children. And the cost of acquiring the level of competence required for full participation in transnational conversation will continue to fall mainly on those doing the learning.

Meanwhile, the pressure of greater interaction across language lines under a *lingua franca* regime will pull the most talented and ambitious in every other language group gradually into an English-speaking environment. Once there is a single language of access to opportunity and power, those who want to shine on the largest stage will strive to perfect their talents in the language of that stage. Those looking for a career in international business or finance or politics will operate increasingly in the *lingua franca*, followed by television producers, news organisations, musicians, essayists, novelists and bloggers who will turn to the *lingua franca* to gain access to the largest market. Their corporate owners or record labels or publishers will push in that direction. A language community can last a long time even under the pressure of such defections, but gradually the rate will increase and the quality of interaction for those left behind deteriorate until the language enters a death spiral. Each individual decision leading to this outcome might well be individually rational, and yet the result be one that is (almost) every community member's least preferred outcome.

The decline of a language community is a loss, not because the loss of a language per se is an injustice, but because the speakers of that language lose the ability to carry on as we can presume they would want to under normal circumstances: participating in, fostering and developing the richness of their own language traditions (Réaume 2000). I do not assume that language cannot change, or that speakers will never choose to leave their language community for another. But the conditions under which those choices are made are morally critical, as are the forces that control those conditions.

Remedying unfairness: compensation versus rectification

Van Parijs recognises (2011, p. 146ff) the unfairness to language communities not lucky enough to have their language selected as the *lingua franca*, and by way of mitigation proposes that, at least in Europe, each indigenous language that meets certain conditions be given a territory within which that language is dominant in the conduct of local affairs.[9] This misunderstands the nature of the unfairness.

His territorialist solution uses local dominance to make up for the fact that another language has the upper hand in inter-group interactions. The idea that this is the best we can do stems from the assumption that convergence on a *lingua franca* is inevitable and beneficial. But if it is not inevitable – and I've suggested reasons for doubt – why should some should have to settle for local status only while another community has both its home turf and the transnational arena as its linguistic terrain? We cannot solve the problem of unequal status in the transnational arena by giving each language group equal status in some *other* domain.

Furthermore, if a *lingua franca* is unnecessary to produce the benefits claimed – like fostering meaningful democratic debate – that leaves mainly the efficiency gains that have been the traditional justification for language integration. In other words, eschewing the pursuit of equal status amongst languages and language communities at the transnational level is not for the sake of democracy, but in order to save money and effort (at least for those already in a position of power).

The central asymmetry remains: that others learn to speak the *lingua franca* and its native speakers do not reciprocate with any other language. The charge of unequal respect arises from this asymmetry. Each language being a queen, 'or at least a "princess"' (Van Parijs 2011, p. 147) somewhere does not address the fundamental issue. In fact, to treat the initial unfairness of this asymmetry as a matter of the cost of language acquisition is odd. Learning a second language no more imposes costs than learning mathematics or history does, though all require effort. Learning is beneficial; normally, the more of it we do the better off we are. This draws us back to the question of why native speakers of the proposed *lingua franca* decline to participate in the benefit of extra language learning and their governments do not provide the opportunity for it, even as these individuals and their governments think it appropriate that others learn *their* language. In the light of the actual history of linguistic domination, this unwillingness also expresses disrespect for other communities. And that is why various policies that try to accord equal respect to language communities do so by promoting active multilingualism, not compensation for loss.

Concluding caveats and cautions

I close with one caveat and a word of advice about the enterprise of moving in the direction of a policy of multilingualism.

The caveat is this: claiming that the loss to a community of the human resource that its language is to them is an injustice does not mean that it must be avoided at all costs. Languages do die out, even without unfair pressure on its speakers to abandon them. And even a history of unfairness may create conditions in which unacceptably Herculean efforts would be required to resuscitate a dying language, or worse, only tyrannical measures would work. I do not favour language survival for its own sake, or at crippling moral or economic cost. I claim only that the first thing that is required is the recognition of equal status of all viable language communities participating in a joint political project.

The details of a sound multilingualism will vary enormously depending on the political, social and demographic details of the situation. Europe is particularly challenging because of the number of official languages to be included as well as the regional languages that do not have official status even internally. Is multilingualism feasible? I can offer no blueprint here. But at the risk of sounding like the died-in-the-wool Marxist who complains that communism has never really been tried, it is clear that multilingualism has mostly never been considered as an option and thus most of the infrastructure it needs has not been attempted. Given the irreversible consequences of a headlong pursuit of a global *lingua franca*, claims about the unfeasibility of multilingualism should not close down argument any more than claims about the unfeasibility of 'greening' our economies should short circuit debate about the need to respond to climate change.

Even if Europe resolved to pursue a multilingualism policy – in practice and not just symbolically – nothing close to full equality of all its official languages could be achieved quickly. This is no excuse not to start. Multilingualism must start with an aspiration that is gradually converted into concrete reality. Institutional and human capacity must be built over time. That perfection cannot be attained immediately is no more reason to abandon the project than the fact that racial integration in the US turned out to be difficult, costly and slow (and remains incomplete) would have been reason to refrain from taking the first steps. After all, universal *lingua franca* competence would also require great effort and expense, especially if we take injustice and inequality seriously. The important questions of language policy start not with what is feasible, but with what is just.

Acknowledgments

I have presented versions of this paper at a colloquium at Nuffield College, Oxford, a Centre for Transnational Legal Studies conference at the University of Turin, as a Law and Philosophy Lecture at the University of Western Ontario, and at the University of Fribourg. I am grateful to participants at all these events for a lively series of discussions. Thanks are also due to Les Green for feedback. This article is a shortened version of one forthcoming in C. Menkel-Meadow, V.V. Ramraj & F. Werro (eds.), *Teaching Transnational Law: Substantive Issues, Pedagogical Approaches*, Ashgate.

Disclosure statement

No potential conflict of interest was reported by the author.

Notes

1. For alternative sketches of these options, see Laitin and Reich (2003, p. 80), and Patten (2007, p. 15).
2. The Canadian experience is similar: after the conquest of New France, the British went to the extraordinary length of deporting much of the French-speaking Acadian population of what is now Nova Scotia (Hodson 2012, Chapter 1). The British also tried, unsuccessfully, as it turned out, to impose English as the language of administration and law in what is now Québec (Cook 1991, pp. 73–81).

3. The overview that follows is drawn from Réaume and Pinto (2012).
4. This argument goes back to J.S. Mill (Gray 1991), but has been reinvigorated recently by Grimm (1995) and Habermas (1995). For other modern explorations of the argument, see Rubio-Marin (2003), Patten (2001), and Van Parijs (2011, pp. 27–31).
5. Van Parijs (2011, p. 26) is explicit about his individualistic focus.
6. Van Parijs seems to take a different view: he assumes, for purposes of determining the level of compensation to those shouldering the burden of second language learning, that the benefit of the existence of a *lingua franca* is measured by the number of new speech partners acquired, rather than the desirability or usefulness of these new opportunities for communication (2011, p. 56). It seems odd to consider it a benefit to me that someone in Tibet has learned English if I will never have reason to want to communicate with that person.
7. Banning dubbing, (Van Parijs 2011, pp. 109–113) aims to make it easier for more people to learn the *lingua franca* more quickly; allowing poaching of English language websites by ESL speakers (pp. 78–81) has a similar rationale. Immersion schooling (pp. 102–106) speeds up the process still further.
8. While Van Parijs acknowledges (2011, p. 94) that the benefits to native speakers include greater influence in communication, he fails fully to explore the resulting injustices.
9. In this, he seems to be taking a leaf out of Jean Laponce's work (1984). Laponce, concerned with the survival of non-dominant language groups, argued that in order to survive, a language needs its own territory within which it is dominant. Van Parijs combines this local strategy with an English unilingualism policy in respect of transnational matters.

Notes on contributor

Denise Réaume is Professor of Law at the University of Toronto and Visiting Professor at the University of Oxford. She has been a keen follower of, and commentator on, Canadian language rights and language policy for many years and has written extensively on language rights, multiculturalism and group rights in respect of both.

References

Cook, R., 1991. Language policy in the Glossophagic state. *In*: D. Schneiderman, ed. *Language and the state: the law and politics of identity.* Cowansville: Les Editions Yvon Blais, 73–81.
Crawford, J., 2000. *At war with diversity: US language policy in an age of anxiety.* Cleveden: Multilingual Matters, Chapter 1.
Grimm, D., 1995. Does Europe need a constitution? *European Law Journal*, 1 (3), 282–302.
Habermas, J., 1995. Remarks on Dieter Grimm's 'Does Europe Need a Constitution?' *European Law Journal*, 1 (3), 303–307.
Hodson, C., 2012. *The Acadian diaspora: an eighteenth century history.* New York: Oxford University Press, Chapter 1.
Laitin, D.D. and Reich, R., 2003. A liberal democratic approach to language justice. *In*: W. Kymlicka and A. Patten, eds. *Language rights and political theory.* Oxford: Oxford University Press, 80–104.
Laponce, J., 1984. *Langue et Territoire.* Québec: Presses de l'université Laval, reprinted in English 1987. *Languages and their territories.* Toronto: University of Toronto Press.

Laws in Wales Act, 1535, 27 Henry VIII (c. 26).

McChesney, R.W. and Nicols, J., 2010. *The death and life of American journalism: the media revolution that will begin the world again.* New York, NY: Nation Books.

Mill, J.S., 1991 [1861]. Considerations on representative government. *In:* J. Gray, ed. *On liberty and other essays.* Oxford: Oxford University Press, 427–434.

Patten, A., 2001. Political theory and language policy. *Political Theory,* 29 (5), 691–715.

Patten, A., 2007. Theoretical foundations of European language debates. *In:* D. Castiglione and C. Longman, eds. *The language question in Europe and diverse societies.* Oxford: Hart, 15–36.

Piatt, B., 1993. *¿Only English?: Law and language policy in the United States.* Albuquerque, NM: University of New Mexico Press, 5–12.

Réaume, D., 1991. Constitutional protection of language: survival or security? *In:* D. Schneiderman, ed. *Language and the state: the law and politics of identity.* Cowansville: Les Editions Yvon Blais, 37–57.

Réaume, D., 1995. Justice between cultures: autonomy and the protection of cultural affiliation. *University of British Columbia Law Review,* 29 (1), 117–142.

Réaume, D., 2000. Official language rights: intrinsic value and the protection of difference. *In:* W. Kymlicka, ed. *Citizenship in diverse societies.* New York: Oxford University Press, 245–272.

Réaume, D. and Pinto, M., 2012. Philosophy of language policy. *In:* B. Spolsky, ed. *The Cambridge handbook of language policy.* Cambridge: Cambridge University Press, 37–58.

Rubio-Marin, R., 2003. Language rights: exploring the competing rationales. *In:* W. Kymlicka and A. Patten, eds. *Language rights and political theory.* Oxford: Oxford University Press, 52–79.

Van Parijs, P., 2003. Linguistic justice. *In:* W. Kymlicka and A. Patten, eds. *Language rights and political theory.* Oxford: Oxford University Press, 153–168.

Van Parijs, P., 2007. Europe's linguistic challenge. *In:* D. Castiglione and C. Longman, eds. *The language question in Europe and diverse societies.* Oxford: Hart, 217–254.

Van Parijs, P., 2011. *Linguistic justice for Europe and for the world.* Oxford: Oxford University Press.

Cooperative justice and English as a lingua franca: the tension between optimism and Anglophones free riding

David Robichaud

Department of Philosophy, University of Ottawa, Ottawa, Canada

In *Linguistic Justice for Europe and for the World,* Philippe Van Parijs proposes three principles of linguistic justice. The first one applies to the fair conditions of the creation of a lingua franca understood as a common good enabling global communication. According to Van Parijs, the actual situation is unfair. The benefits are distributed evenly among speakers mastering English, but the costs are born entirely by those investing resources in learning English as a second language. I want to challenge this argument and point to a dilemma in Van Parijs' proposition. He can either accept that English as global lingua franca (EGLF) is a done deal such that only "apocalyptical events" could prevent English from becoming the first global lingua franca, in which case he will have to make peace with the fact that Anglophones can enjoy the benefits this produces without having to make any kind of contribution. Or, he can temper his optimism, find reasons why natural interactions could fail at producing EGLF so as to convince native Anglophones that without their contribution, without some form of an investment in the creation of EGLF, it will not happen, or at least, it will not happen in a way that is maximally beneficial to them. I propose some arguments pointing to some benefits that would only be accessible to native Anglophones through cooperation and therefore through contributing to the creation of EGLF. Without such an argument, native Anglophones are free to benefit from the impressive by-product of the decisions to learn English of all those interested to improve their social and economic prospects: a global lingua franca.

In *Linguistic Justice*, Philippe Van Parijs proposes three principles of justice that should be applied in order to produce just outcomes related to language. More precisely, he begins by arguing in favor of the creation of a lingua franca for Europe and for the world. Such a global tool would allow people to communicate across the world and would increase peoples' utility in many ways. This is not however the main reason for accelerating the spread of English as a lingua franca. There are more important reasons. The first one is that this global language will create a global justificatory community. The second one is that it will contribute to make the distribution of wealth from the rich to the least well off politically feasible. The rationally appealing ideal of a just world justifies the creation of a tool, a global lingua franca, that would contribute to changing people's intuitions about their duties of international and global justice.

For reasons of efficiency, we should not try to make a "neutral" or "impartial" choice of language. It will necessarily be the language of some, and in this situation, we might as well pick the language that is already the most spoken and the one learnt by the most people in the world: English. Proposing the spread of English as a lingua franca will of course create situations of injustices. The two most important according to Van Parijs are inequalities of opportunities, since Anglophones will be dominant in terms of skills and fluency in English as global lingua franca (EGLF), reaping huge comparative benefits. There are also inequalities of status, or disparity of esteem, that will be created by adopting the language of some nations as *the* global language. Van Parijs proposes some very interesting and very controversial remedies to these inequalities.

What I want to discuss is the first principle of justice proposed, one that is not discussed as often as the others, and one that even Van Parijs sees as the least important: the principle of cooperative justice. This principle does not apply to the situation after EGLF has been created but rather to the very conditions under which this common good can be created fairly.

The idea is simple and intuitive. Everyone learning English will benefit from their investment by getting access not only to Anglophone countries, but to the whole world. The relative benefits will vary depending on the size of the community one belongs to, the opportunities one really has to use this newly learnt language, etc. But some people, those already mastering English, the native Anglophones especially, are getting a free ride: they get the benefits of having this same access to the world, without having to bear any cost in the creation of EGLF. Due to network externalities, every new speaker joining the English community not only gets access to those Anglophones, but offers an extra speaker to all those already mastering English. Van Parijs considers that this free ride is problematic and that it is a case of injustice. I want to challenge this claim. I will try to argue that it is not a case of free riding, at least not without another argument to show how native Anglophones would benefit from cooperation leading to a specific form of EGLF.

Freedom in cooperation

'Cooperative interactions' are interactions of a very specific form, distinct from what we will call 'natural interactions'. Natural interactions are simple interactions where each individual chooses his most promising strategy, an equilibrium strategy, the one offering the best expected utility considering other agent's expected strategy. The best examples can be found in the market. Each individual makes decisions as to what work to do, how many hours to work, what to sell or buy and at what price, etc. Every decision is based on an attempt to maximize individual utility. There is no cooperation, and in fact, we forbid some forms of common strategies like those leading to monopolistic positions within the market.

In a perfect market, one's freedom and pursuit of utility maximization is only constrained by one's preferences, talents, virtues and purchasing power. Such freedom leads to optimal collective results, that is, everyone is as happy as he could be following self-interested production and transactions. Every mutually advantageous transaction has theoretically been completed, and those that have not, have not precisely because they were not interesting to at least one person in the deal. One cannot complain about one's situation since this is the best situation one could obtain considering one's own and others' capacities and preferences. This is a situation where liberty, equality and efficiency coincide.

In real markets, utility functions are not always independent, that is, some agents' actions influence other people's utility. The influence can be positive or negative. The negative costs produced by an agent and involuntarily imposed on others are called negative externalities (e.g. pollution); the positive costs are called positive externalities (e.g. the pleasure my neighbors get by looking at my garden). These costs and benefits do not modify substantially the utility of the agent producing them, and therefore, they are not taken into account in the calculation of utility maximizing behaviors. However, once pooled, these costs and benefits can amount to huge collective costs and benefits.

These externalities represent both problems for efficiency and morality. The efficiency problem is that individual choices will produce more pollution and less gardens than we would collectively prefer. To get to an optimal situation, we must internalize the externalities, that is, we must make sure that agents bear the total costs and get total benefits of their actions. The morality problem concerns only negative externalities. The problem with externalities is that some of the costs of an agent's choice are unilaterally imposed on others. It is a violation of their freedom and equality. We should then forbid these behaviors or require compensation for those suffering from them. But positive externalities do not pose any moral problem. Each individual acts in ways that are judged to be rationally beneficial, and the external goods produced are only a gift offered to others. What is wrong with free gardens? The only problem related with positive externalities is that the kind of behaviors producing them will not be as ubiquitous as they should be if the externalities were internalized, if the agents received every benefit they produce.

This is particularly relevant for our argument, since network externalities are a special type of positive externalities. When we learn English, we create benefits for every other user of English through the creation of economies of scale for products in English but also through the expansion of an existing network of speakers. We all expect benefits from learning a language and that is why we invest in such a demanding project. But we also create benefits, adding an extra speaker, to the whole community of Anglophones. Since we do not benefit from the utility produced for others, it will not influence our decision to learn or not a language. In some cases, public goods will not be produced, here a lingua franca, since the benefits enjoyed by people investing in the learning will not be sufficient to motivate them.[1]

Without any externality or other market failure, natural interactions produce the best collective results. But in other cases, each individual choosing his maximizing strategy leads to collective problems and everybody is then better off following one collective strategy offering optimal results.

We can think of problems of *coordination*, like the side of the road on which to drive. If each individual chooses his preferred side, this will lead to chaos. This is of course in nobody's interest, and it is therefore rational for everyone to collectively choose a strategy, like 'everyone drives on the right', instead of letting each individual choose a strategy. This collective strategy will make everyone better off, and it is therefore rational for every individual to constrain his freedom, to agree not to follow an individual strategy. Once a collective strategy is chosen, individuals have a duty to follow the rule and comply with the collective strategy.

When we face problems of coordination, it is easy to find collective strategy that people will rationally agree to follow since there is no benefit for anyone breaking the rule. The situation is not as simple with cases of *cooperation*. Cooperation is also a way to produce optimal results in situations wherein individuals selecting their own best strategies lead to collective problems. Once again, individuals rationally agree to a common strategy that everyone is expected to follow in order to avoid collective catastrophes. The only problem is that, while the collective result produced by each agent sticking to the collective strategy is better than the situation wherein each agent chooses an equilibrium strategy, in these cases, there is however an even better possibility: letting others create the collective benefit and follow the collective strategy while being the only one to follow a maximizing strategy.

The paradigmatic problem of cooperation is the prisoner's dilemma. Two criminals are interrogated for a bank robbery. The police have no proof against them, but caught them with a firearm, which is enough to sentence them to 3 years in prison. They have an offer for the criminals:

> As it is you are in for three years in prison. If you confirm that your partner in crime committed the robbery, if you collaborate and create the proofs to sentence him to ten years of prison, we will take three years off your sentence and will let you go. However, if he also confirms that you were there, you will both get seven years of prison, that is, ten years each for armed robbery minus the three years for collaboration with the police.

If each prisoner chooses the best individual strategy available, the one offering the best expected benefit, each will denounce the other. Why? Because whatever the other does, each prisoner is better off denouncing him. If they both denounce, they each get seven instead of ten years, if one denounces the other and the other remains silent, then one walks away instead of spending three years in jail. From an individual perspective, the best strategy is obvious: denounce! From a collective perspective, the outcome is the worst possible: fourteen years of prison collectively.

This is a clear case where cooperation provides a solution in order to increase everyone's utility. By choosing a collective strategy and by acting upon it, it is possible to produce a situation where each individual is better off (3 years each instead of 7), and in which the collective outcome is optimal (the lowest total number of years in jail). The problem with cooperation is that once we agree to a norm, to a collective strategy, it is beneficial to break our agreement and act following our best individual strategy. In this case, 3 years in jail is better than 7, and even though a rule among criminals not to denounce each other offers optimal collective results, it is always beneficial for each individual to break the rule and follow his interest.

There is no a priori duty not to denounce, no natural obligation to cooperate. The duty is created by the agreement of self-interested prisoners trying to avoid an undesirable result. If, for some reason, a prisoner prefers not to cooperate (suppose he wants to get back in jail or he is a member of a powerful criminal gang and knows that nobody would denounce him fearing to be killed), he is doing nothing wrong. What is wrong is not to refuse cooperation when we can expect better payoff following our best individual strategy, but refusing to follow a collective strategy we agreed to for the expected benefits it makes possible. The distinction between refusing cooperation due to insufficient expected benefits and agreeing to cooperate but violating the rule must be maintained if we want to maintain the individual's freedom. Van Parijs identified explicitly the need to reconcile freedom, justice and efficiency in any attempt to find a normative criterion of cooperative justice in the creation of EGLF.[2] This requirement is lost in the formulation of the argument proposed in *Linguistic Justice for Europe and for the World*. Considering that cooperation is mandatory each time a collective good can be produced, without any consideration of the marginal benefits offered to individuals creating and benefiting from it, amounts to allowing some to constrain others into cooperation.

In order to determine if Anglophones are acting in a morally reprehensible way, we must ask the following question: Are they refusing a cooperative agreement since they get a better payoff by remaining in a context of natural interactions, which is not morally wrong, or are they selfishly going back on their word and refusing to act according to a collective strategy that offers better payoffs to every agent involved, including themselves? In the first case, they remain free to benefit from their advantageous linguistic position; in the second, they are free riding and exploiting others by not contributing to the creation of the lingua franca.

Two criteria of rational cooperation

Some collective goods cannot be produced unless people agree to abandon their quest for utility maximization and agree to constrain their choice of strategies in order to choose a single collective strategy. The goods produced by this general agreement make up the cooperative surplus, that is, the surplus that would not have been produced by natural interactions. Agents will rationally agree to constrain their freedom only if such a surplus is produced and if they wish for it to be produced.

Of course an explicit agreement is not necessary to trigger duties of cooperation. All we need is to demonstrate that cooperation improves everyone's situation when compared to natural interactions. Two criteria must be met in order to conclude that cooperation is in every individual's interest and that constraints on their behaviors are morally justified: *internal rationality* and *external rationality*. The criterion of internal rationality tries to identify the rational way to distribute the benefits produced by cooperation. We need a principle according to which we can distribute the cooperative surplus in a way that is rationally acceptable for every member of cooperation, and then, we can consider that this distribution is fair and morally acceptable. Van Parijs proposes an equal ratio of costs to benefits, that is, people should get a share of the cooperative surplus proportional to their contribution. We will not discuss this criterion and will consider it acceptable.

The main problem is that Van Parijs does not apply the second criterion of external rationality. Agreeing on a rational way to distribute the cooperative surplus is not the only issue that agents are interested in. More fundamentally, they want to know if cooperation improves their situation *when compared to a counterfactual* where individuals only interact, where individuals choose their best available individual strategy. It is absolutely necessary to maintain the possibility not to cooperate in cases where cooperation offers no improvement over the benefits we can expect from natural interactions. Nothing less than freedom is at stake if we do not take external rationality seriously.

By simply showing that Anglophones benefit from the world population learning English, we cannot conclude that there is cooperation to which Anglophones thus have a duty to contribute. If those benefits are externalities produced by a large number of individuals freely and rationally choosing to learn English as a maximizing strategy, native Anglophones are doing nothing wrong by benefiting from it. However, if the benefits produced were only possible through the cooperation of all, or if compensation from native Anglophones were necessary to make the learning rationally advantageous for learners of EGLF, then a contribution to the production of this good would be morally required.

Is EGLF a cooperative surplus or a collective action benefit? Turning Van Parijs' data against him

To show that EGLF is a collective action benefit and not a cooperative surplus, we will use Van Parijs' account of the spread of English. How did it happen, and what can we expect for the future?

The counterfactual situation we can expect without cooperation is not one of global monolingualism,[3] but rather one where 'the learning of English all over the world [...] is happening [...] on a grand scale, powerfully driven by the individual and collective self-interest of hundreds of millions of people' (Van Parijs 2012, p. 77). Self-interest suffices to motivate a large portion of the world population to invest in learning English, and this is without any collective or cooperative strategy. The relevant counterfactual to cooperation is natural interaction, that is, a situation wherein each individual decides for himself what strategy is most likely to maximize his utility. This counterfactual is therefore the rise of English as a global second language, a situation in which the best individual strategy considered in the light of other people's expected strategy, is learning English as a second language. Not monolingualism. There are different reasons explaining how we arrived at a situation in which it is in people's interest to learn English, and there are reasons to expect this situation to persist.

At the beginning of the book, Van Parijs explains why 'it is English and English alone that can reasonably claim to have become a global lingua franca'. He mentions two types of explanations that have nothing to do with any kind of superiority of the language itself. First, socio- and psycho-linguistics micro-mechanisms; and second, historical events.

Van Parijs presents two micro-mechanisms playing a role in the linguistic choices made by people. First, learning a language is *probability-driven*. Learning a language is made more appealing when the probability of having to speak it is high. We get more motivated when we can expect many interactions in this language. This also operates at another level, since learning a language is also made easier when we have many opportunities to speak it.

This first micro-mechanism is accompanied by another, making it work exponentially in favor of English: maxi-min language use. In multilingual groups, conversations happen most often in what Van Parijs presents as the maxi-min language: the language 'of maximal minimal competence' (Van Parijs 2012, p. 14). We tend to prefer to minimize exclusion in contexts of multilingual interactions. The more widespread a language becomes, the most likely it becomes that it will be the maxi-min language, increasing therefore the probability to speak it and the motivation to learn it and the opportunities to practice it. The two micro-mechanisms create a 'virtuous circle' and their effects compound and contribute exponentially to the status of English as a global lingua franca.

The second type of explanation has to do with morally arbitrary historical events. The spread of English is explained by the success and failures of linguistic communities within the global sphere, not by any recognition of its superiority over other languages. Language policies and population movements have been driven by wars and international politics, and through many turns of events this morally arbitrary historical process contributed to the status of English as the global lingua franca.

Van Parijs links the two types of explanatory factors,

> Events of this sort do not obliterate the socio-linguistic dynamics, but define parameters within which it operates. They provide a background for the relentless work of the micro-mechanisms described above. The [micro-mechanisms'] cumulative interaction in a high-mobility, intense-communicative world, has snowballed English into a European and universal lingua franca position from which it could be dislodged only by some unforeseeable apocalyptic event – or by a concerted and persistent Europe-wide or worldwide endeavor to block or reverse the convergence process just analyzed. (Van Parijs 2012, pp. 23–24)

Van Parijs presents these arguments in a passage where he tries to convince us that it is realistic to hope for the creation of a global lingua franca, since it is already happening, and that the language that we should promote to play this important role is English. The problem we raise is contained in the passage just quoted. These factors not only explain what happened, but they predict what we can expect. Only apocalyptic events could stop or reverse the process of English becoming a global lingua franca.

Choosing between optimism and moral condemnation

If Van Parijs is right to be optimistic about the prospect of English becoming a global lingua franca, and about the trend accelerating in learning English, then he must be wrong about the native Anglophones' (morally problematic) free riding. In the present situation, individuals and institutions are pursuing their best self-interest, following a strategy they see as utility maximizing. The aggregate outcome of all those strategies leads to the acquisition of linguistic capital at the personal level, and to the creation of a huge network of potential communication that benefits each member at the aggregate level due to network externalities. Individuals all across the world, as well as States interested to promote the human capital of their populations, see English not only as the best language but as one of the best skills to maximize their utility. They get benefits even without contributions from native Anglophones, and on this basis, we can expect that the latter are not interested in subsidizing individuals in order to promote a motivation they already have. People invest in some individual human capital, and as a by-product of a multitude of such decisions, a global lingua franca benefiting native Anglophones is being created.

If that was the end of the story, we could not blame native Anglophones of free riding. However, we might have reasons to be more pessimistic than Van Parijs about the irreversibility of the spread of EGLF. Pessimism could create doubts on the prospects of the creation of a *desirable form of* lingua franca and could then justify rationally a contribution from native Anglophones in order to ensure the creation of a communicative tool offering them important expected utilities. If individual strategies of utility maximization lead to collective suboptimal results, then we could collectively decide to adopt a collective strategy that would constrain members' behaviors and that would make a contribution mandatory for anyone reaping benefits from cooperation. Van Parijs recognizes the need to show that it is in native Anglophones' interest to produce a lingua franca. However, he does so in order to make it feasible to hope for a tax to be collected from them. In reality, it is the very moral duty of Anglophones to pay such a tax, not just their willingness to abide by this duty, which depends on their interest in adopting a collective strategy.

How could we convince native Anglophones that it is in their best self-interest to contribute to the creation of EGLF by offering compensation to the learners?

(1) Linguistic competition

We could first imagine another language surpassing English as the most widespread, useful language, the one that people choose and learn following micro-mechanisms of probability-sensitive learning and maxi-min dynamics. Once a language becomes an interesting option for enough people, the micro-mechanisms contribute to make it even more appealing to others and to make it the language used in the most plurilingual contexts. If such a scenario is expected, or if there is simply a weak probability for this happening in the future, then Anglophones should intervene and contribute to the spread of English for rational and interested reasons.

I think Van Parijs is right when he argues that the situation is already irreversible. We might not see the day where humanity shares a global lingua franca, but if we do, English will probably be it. As he mentions, 'no other language, whether at European level or worldwide, gives any sign of rivaling English as a universal lingua franca, and the snowball effect currently unfolding is such that one can safely predict that no language will ever do' (Van Parijs 2012, p. 22). This should convince only pessimistic native Anglophones to subsidize learning.

(2) An elitist Lingua Franca

We could imagine that not enough people choose to learn English (elitist lingua franca), or that, most people do not choose to learn enough of it in order to produce optimal results (weak democratic lingua franca). The presence of network externalities could lead to such a situation: without compensation, many people will not receive enough benefits to motivate them to learn English. In the first scenario, we end up with an elitist version of the lingua franca, allowing complex and specialized conversations between people from different linguistic communities but requiring translation to bring these conversations to the people. In the second scenario, people learn English and develop a passive knowledge giving them access to cultural products and to information, and only a limited active knowledge that does not allow a global deliberation or a global debate on political or social matters in a shared language.

This would obviously represent a problem for Van Parijs, and the reasons why he proposes the acceleration of EGLF, namely the creation of a demos and making global justice more feasible. But Van Parijs does not ground the duty to subsidize learning on a duty of distributive justice. He grounds it on the alleged cooperative surplus from which Anglophones benefit. The question is then: Would they benefit more if the lingua franca created was a more democratic one? Is it in their interest to agree to cooperate in order to increase global proficiency in English?

It is far from obvious. As Van Parijs mentions, it is only an approximation that every new speaker adds a utility of 1 to people already mastering English. Many variables modify this benefit. In fact, we could almost propose another approximation: each additional speaker offers decreasing marginal utility. We want many meaningful and interesting speech partners. But we do not want as many speech partners as possible, no matter whom or where they are and without considering what they have to offer. It seems plausible to imagine a threshold at which new speakers – including native Anglophones – cease to add enough value to the existing linguistic community to justify subsidizing their learning. Van Parijs mentions that small communities get more benefits from learning English than large communities do. This also applies to Anglophones. Once they have access to elites worldwide, once they can expect to be able to travel and find people speaking English in most of the countries they wish to visit, the benefits offered by each new speaker might be insignificant whereas the costs of learning will remain more or less constant. It is doubtful that native Anglophones would want to subsidize the learning of English as long as there are learners, but it is still reasonable to imagine that some compensation could be in the interest of native Anglophones in order to ensure enough people will invest in EGLF.

(3) Babelization of English

Another plausible scenario susceptible to attract native Anglophones' attention is the *babelization* of English. In a recent book dedicated to the study of World Englishes and of English in a global context, Philip Seargeant identifies two challenges facing the rise of English as an international language allowing global communication. The first one has already been discussed at length by

Van Parijs: How English as a global language can avoid increasing global inequalities. The second however is left unexplored by Van Parijs: 'how a language which has diverse varieties all around the globe can be drawn upon to function efficiently as a stable medium of communication' (Seargeant 2012, p. 87). The difference between an error and an innovation in English is more complex than for other languages due to the absence of linguistic authority like the *Académie Française* for French. Deviation from standards will be recognized following interrelated measures and factors like how, where and by whom it is used.[4] With more people with English as a second language than as a native language, deviations from standards will be more numerous and much harder to track and evaluate. The recent and rich literature on 'Englishes' and 'Globish' makes clear that the creation of a global lingua franca requires more than a multitude of individuals learning and using, at least approximately, a common second language. Some norms will be necessary in order to ensure that EGLF remains intelligible across the globe especially if it is to fulfill formal and complex communicative roles.

This babelization could be the natural result of linguistic practices left without 'oversight' or it could be the outcome of language planning. Partially isolated local practices will tend to distance themselves over time, and deviations from standard use could begin to be seen as innovations in different parts of the English world.

We could also imagine that some nations decide to invest in English, but that they decide to shape it to their identity, preferences or needs. They could then import many local idioms, adapt grammar rules from local languages, prefer some pronunciations to others, etc. They could decide to shape English to their liking, either for practical reasons or for ideological reasons. Of course this would make English easier for local people to use and learn, but it would also make it closer to their identity, further from standard English associated with the USA and UK and what they stand for.

The whole debate about teaching English as a Foreign Language or Lingua Franca English helps us understand the different paths EGLF could take. Should we prefer a diluted version of English as spoken in Anglophone nations, or rather a disincarnated version of global English colored by multiple local practices? We don't have time to get into this debate, but one thing is clear: some coordination is going to be necessary if we want to avoid a more or less damaging babelization of EGLF. Native Anglophones could be tempted to offer to coordinate learning in order to ensure that the final product, EGLF, offers intelligibility and is maximally beneficial for them. Interestingly enough, one efficient way to do so would be to offer cultural products such as movies, music and books, produced in Anglophone nations, to non-Anglophone freely or at low cost. Van Parijs proposes to counter the free riding from native Anglophones by a retaliatory free riding: poaching the web! In face of the native Anglophones benefiting from EGLF without contributing, non-Anglophones should consume cultural products from native Anglophones without any consideration of intellectual property. For Van Parijs, this poaching of the web is justified as a compensatory free riding, but we could rather consider it as a contribution from Anglophones in order to maximize the benefits they can expect from the creation of EGLF. They could agree to give a free access to their cultural products in order to influence the creation of a certain type of collective good, a form of EGLF that maximizes their benefits.

(4) Popular opposition to English

In a short passage, Van Parijs mentions that there can be deviations from what the micro-mechanisms would 'recommend'. Other criteria can be used to select a language. In some cases, this is intended as a way to promote learning, but in other cases, this is done for symbolic, ideological or political reasons. One could refuse to learn English, or refuse to speak it in certain contexts, in an attempt to dissociate oneself from it. We could therefore imagine scenarios where English would stop being the obvious maxi-min choice, where the micro-mechanisms are slowed down or blocked in some contexts.

We could imagine an ideological posture taken against the USA or the UK. A rejection of their ideology, of their identity and of what they stand for, could convince a substantial portion of the population not to learn English, or at least not to use it in some contexts. Many authors for example think that the identity and the ideology of Anglophone countries follow the spread of their language. It is plausible to imagine a proportion of the global population rejecting English for such reasons, especially in more formal contexts where the symbolic significance of political decisions can be very important. We could also imagine English no longer being 'cool' and many people refraining from using it naturally in informal contexts. A contribution from native speakers could improve others' perception of these communities, which are often seen as self-centered, neo-liberal and hesitant to cooperate. Van Parijs is right when he mentions that we can produce good arguments showing that a language is not intrinsically linked to an ideology, and I agree that it is important to reassert that English was chosen for pragmatic reasons, not for moral or linguistic superiority ones. However, my argument is empirical: no matter how conceptually wrong they are, we can still imagine a large number of individuals rejecting English as a way to reject the ideology and behavior of its native speakers.

(5) Cooperation beyond EGLF

We might finally imagine that native Anglophones consider themselves part of a wider cooperative venture. One that is not restricted to building a lingua franca, but of maintaining institutional stability on economic, social and political fronts. They could look at the bigger picture and see the lingua franca as part of a larger scheme of cooperation, and although the cooperation to create or accelerate the spread of EGLF is not in their interest, they still have an interest in maintaining a good reputation in international relations. This brings us back to the father-in-law example. Van Parijs mentions that it would be wrong for the Anglophones not to contribute to the creation of EGLF just as it would be wrong for him not to contribute to the cleaning of the house during his stay at his father-in-law's. Even though the father-in-law cleans way before Van Parijs feels it needs to be done, and even though he does it out of self-interest, it would be morally condemnable not to contribute or compensate the father-in-law.

It is not the fact that Van Parijs and his family benefit from the father-in-law (let's not say obsessive) cleaning that creates a duty to reciprocate or to share the burden of that cleaning. Since Van Parijs does not enjoy most of the benefits the cleaning produces, he could decide to remain in a natural interaction, to refuse cooperation, without doing anything wrong. However, families are very thick groups of cooperation from which we get large complex benefits. In this case, Van Parijs is not afraid the cleaning will not be done if he does not contribute to the cooperation, he is simply afraid that his father-in-law or other people around will react negatively if he does not contribute. It is not the benefits from the cleaning enjoyed by all that creates a duty of contribution for the Van Parijs, it is rather being members of a particular, general and very complex cooperative scheme.

The same could apply to native Anglophones, especially for UK citizens who are engaged in a thick web of cooperation through their membership in the European Union. If we look at the thick web of cooperation EU countries are involved in, we could consider that it is the benefits offered by this "general" cooperative venture, not those offered by a specific one, namely the creation of EGLF, that triggers a duty to contribute. If it is in the interest of native Anglophones to remain good co-operators in the cooperative ventures they are involved in, it could be in their interest to contribute to the creation of EGLF.

Conclusion

Philippe Van Parijs is stuck with a dilemma. He can either accept that EGLF is a done deal such that only 'apocalyptical events' could prevent English from becoming the first global lingua franca, in which case he will have to make peace with the fact that Anglophones can enjoy the benefits this produces without having to make any kind of contribution. Or, he can temper his optimism, find reasons why natural interactions could fail at producing EGLF so as to convince native Anglophones that without their contribution, without some form of an investment in the creation of EGLF, it will not happen, or at least, it will not happen in a way that is maximally beneficial to them. I tried to propose some arguments pointing to some benefits that would be accessible only to native Anglophones through cooperation and therefore through contributing to the creation of EGLF. Without such an argument, native Anglophones are free to benefit from the impressive by-product of the decisions to learn English of all those interested to improve their social and economic prospects: a global lingua franca.

Disclosure statement

No potential conflict of interest was reported by the author.

Notes

1. Church and King (1993).
2. Van Parijs (2003) and Van Parijs and De Briey (2002).
3. In the second chapter, Van Parijs proposes to consider the cooperative surplus as the benefits unavailable in a context of universal unilingualism. This chapter presents only simplified situations and leave aside many details regarding the reality of linguistic interactions. We cannot be sure that Van Parijs proposes universal monolingualism as a counterfactual, but some passages support such a position (i.e. p. 63).
4. Ayo Bamgbose (1998) proposes 5 interrelated measures to discriminate innovations from errors: (1) Demographic (is it used by L1 speakers); (2) Geographical (how widely has it spread); (3) Authoritative (what is the social status of those using it); (4) Codification (where is the usage sanctioned); and (5) Acceptability (what are the attitudes of users and non-users towards this usage). Quoted in Li (2010, p. 627).

Notes on contributor

David Robichaud is an assistant professor in Moral and Political Philosophy at the University of Ottawa. He works on linguistic justice, on contractarianism and on trust in multicultural societies.

References

Bamgbose, A., 1998. Torn between the norms: innovations in world Englishes. *World Englishes*, 17 (1), 1–14.
Church, J. and King, I., 1993. Bilingualism and Network Externalities. *The Canadian Journal of Economics*, 26, 337–345.
Li, D.C.S., 2010. When does an unconventional form becomes an innovation. *In*: A. Kirkpatrick, ed. *The Routledge handbook of world Englishes*. New York: Routledge, 617–633.
Seargeant, P., 2012. *Exploring world Englishes. Language in a global context*. New York: Routledge.
Van Parijs, P., 2003. Linguistic justice. *In*: W. Kymlicka and A. Patten, eds. *Language rights and political theory*. Oxford: Oxford University Press, 152–168.
Van Parijs, P., 2012. *Linguistic justice for Europe and for the world*. Oxford: Oxford University Press.
Van Parijs, P. and De Briey, L., 2002. La justice linguistique comme justice cooperative. *Revue de Philosophie Économique*, 5, 5–38.

Language, dignity, and territory

Anna Stilz

Department of Politics, Princeton University, Princeton, NJ, USA

This article raises two critical concerns about Philippe Van Parijs's recent book. First, I argue that Van Parijs lacks a convincing account of why global English poses a threat to parity of esteem for other linguistic communities. I argue that English threatens the dignity of speakers of other languages only because background power inequalities are driving its adoption. Second, I question whether linguistic territoriality is the right way to restore parity of esteem. I show that official multilingualism provides a superior approach to managing linguistic heterogeneity.

Philippe Van Parijs believes that justice requires an egalitarian distribution of options and life-prospects across the globe. Specifically, he favors a world in which a universal basic income is distributed to each human being, and the value of that income is set at a level that sustainably maximizes the opportunities of the globally least well off. Any departures from this distribution can be justified only as a result of preferences and choices for which people can properly be held responsible (Van Parijs 1995, p. 228, Van Parijs 2011, p. 88 – hereafter cited parenthetically by page number).

This is a demanding conception of global justice, and revolutionary changes will be needed before its implementation becomes a realistic possibility. Domestic economic policy must be constrained by global institutions that can tax, regulate international finance and trade, and enforce socioeconomic justice transnationally. We must do away with border controls that fetter free movement, allowing those born in Nigeria to access all the options and opportunities available in Norway. We will need to build structures of deliberation and electoral accountability that can facilitate representative government at the world level, possibly re-imagining our conception of democracy in the process. We can expect our current configuration of states, territories, and collective identities to be radically transformed by this undertaking.

Of course, many people do not wish to transform their existing political institutions in this way. But for Van Parijs, this provides no good argument against making these changes. Instead, 'feelings ought to be shaped by just institutions. They ought not to dictate which institutions should be regarded as just' (Van Parijs 2007, p. 644). Our current political institutions and patterns of social solidarity are not of intrinsic value in themselves: they are instruments for the pursuit of justice, and we should not hesitate to refashion these tools if justice so demands. 'Nations, politically organized peoples, are not part of the ethical framework of global egalitarian justice. They are sheer instruments to be created and dismantled, structured and absorbed, empowered and con-strained, in the service of justice ...' (p. 139). As a prudent political thinker, however, Van Parijs recognizes that this reform project ought not to be attempted all at once, in top-down fashion. Instead, it should be undertaken through a series of incremental steps. A good start, he claims, is the establish-ment of regional organizations such as the EU, which might eventually serve us as a model for building a future transnational demos and its associated global institutions (p. 27).

Unlike Van Parijs, I am not a global egalitarian. But I will not question that account of distributive justice here. Global egalitarianism is a widely supported position, and so its implications are worth exploring. Moreover, what is par-ticularly fascinating in Van Parijs's project is his treatment of how we might justly transition to a future global egalitarian arrangement. He distinguishes himself from other cosmopolitans by offering us a much more systematic attempt to theorize the moral challenges that are raised by his theory's imple-mentation. Must everyone in the world assimilate to the same language, in order to access equivalent economic opportunities? Will all people need to undergo a standard Western education, abandoning their traditional occupations and cultural pursuits? If the emerging global culture is inflected by American or European culture, do those from other backgrounds have a morally serious complaint about having to forgo collective identities they would prefer to sus-tain? Finally, if building a global political community will forseeably lead to the extinction of many people's cultural identities, does that provide us any reason to refrain from creating it, or to go about its establishment more cautiously and circumspectly than we otherwise might have?

In *Linguistic Justice for Europe and for the World*, Van Parijs investigates these issues through the lens of global language policy. He offers us a some-what ambiguous, even Janus-faced, account of just global egalitarian reform. In discussing these issues, Van Parijs allows that justice may have more than one dimension: the familiar dimension of egalitarian distribution, on the one hand, and another 'dimension of justice that is irreducible to the equalization of opportunities', which he calls *parity of esteem*: 'in a just society, people must not be stigmatized, despised, disparaged, or humiliated because of their collective identity' (p. 119). We ought not to transition to a globally just dis-tribution of opportunities, then, in a way that violates parity of esteem, by insulting or humiliating people's existing collective identities.

I think Van Parijs is right to highlight this additional 'parity of esteem' dimension of justice. But this sets up a dilemma for his overall view. If justice has two distinct components – the equal distribution of opportunities, on the one hand, and parity of esteem, on the other – is not it possible that these two components might systematically diverge from one another, pulling us in different directions? Which element of justice ought we to prioritize in such a case? Could it even be – in the extreme – that the strict observance of justice in one form (parity of esteem) could prohibit us from realizing justice in the other form (distributive equality)? Van Parijs himself recognizes this worry and briefly considers it (pp. 204–206), though he does not believe the tradeoff will be as sharp as I have posed it here.

This potential tension between the two dimensions of justice is reflected in Van Parijs's prescriptions for global language policy. On the one hand, he is an enthusiastic proponent of expanding the use of English as a lingua franca in Europe and around the world. Global English, for him, is a vehicle for forging the ties of communication and solidarity upon which a European and – eventually – a world *demos* might come into existence. In that sense, it is demanded by distributive justice. Indeed, 'people committed to egalitarian global justice should not only welcome the spread of English as a lingua franca but see it as their duty to contribute to this spread in Europe and throughout the world (p. 31)'.

At the same time, Van Parijs gives a sympathetic hearing to complaints that this dominance of English represents an injustice to speakers of other languages. While skeptical of claims that there are fundamental rights to the survival of one's own language or that linguistic diversity is itself of intrinsic value (p. 146), he considers three other ways in which a complaint of linguistic injustice could be compellingly formulated: (1) in terms of *unfair cooperation*, (2) in terms of *inequality of opportunity*, and (3) in terms of *unequal esteem*.

I want to focus here on the third formulation, since it is the one that implicates the distinct dimension of justice as parity of esteem. (The other two complaints, I believe, can be fully characterized in terms of egalitarian distributive justice; indeed, addressing them requires accelerating the spread and diffusion of global English). In treating this third complaint, Van Parijs ultimately concludes that it is just to promote English as a global lingua franca only if, alongside it, we at the same time introduce a territorially differentiated linguistic regime that allows non-English speakers to coercively protect their languages, by making them the official languages of a political territory. Such a regime is required in order to counteract the threat of unequal respect that the increasing dominance of English poses to speakers of these other tongues.

But why exactly does the global use of English pose a threat of unequal respect? To illustrate the idea, Van Parijs tells the story of a Flemish waiter in Bruges who indignantly refuses to serve a customer ordering his beer in French. The waiter objects to the customer's arrogant assumption that it is French, not Dutch, that should structure their interaction. And Van Parijs claims that 'when this happens systematically ... it can easily lend itself to an interpretation analogous to a situation in which it is always the members of the same caste or gender that need to bow when meeting members of the other' (p. 119). Speakers of other languages might interpret the global use of English similarly, as a slight to their native tongue and, by extension, to themselves.

But would these speakers be *correct* to see English's global precedence as an insult to them? I don't deny the pull of the intuition that the Flemish waiter is rightly indignant. But do officials of the EU Parliament, or the attendees at an international conference, have a similar complaint when proceedings are conducted in English? The question is particularly pressing because if Van Parijs's explanation of the factors driving the global spread of English is true, then *no insult is intended*. I can imagine perceiving others' refusal to interact in my native language as insulting if I have reason to think it arises from a belief in the inferiority of my language, or of the people who speak it. But for Van Parijs, these 'colonial' attitudes are not driving the global rise of English. Instead, English's spread is explained by a set of rational microdynamics that make it advantageous for individuals to communicate in English when they need to interact with a linguistically diverse group of people. According to Van Parijs, English systematically tends to be the *maxi-min language*, the language that is known best by those who are least skilled at communication outside their native tongue. For this reason, it is the most efficient vehicle of communication in diverse multilingual settings. People opt for English not because they think it is intrinsically superior, but because it is to everyone's advantage to speak it in transnational interactions.

If this is right, though, then why does the choice of English in transnational settings insult or humiliate the speakers of other languages? We might compare it with an analogous situation of rational convergence on a common standard (p. 16): as more people begin to use Word rather than Word Perfect, it becomes rational for me to adopt Word as well, even if I otherwise prefer Word Perfect (because I am more familiar with it, or like its user-friendly features). Surely it would seem ridiculous for me, however, to claim a threat to my equal dignity in this! So why is convergence on a lingua franca different?

Of course, a language can be distinguished from a word processing program along several dimensions, and these differences may be relevant to the dignity complaint. First, it is much harder to switch languages than it is to switch computer programs. Second, the choice of a language – unlike a word processor – is often imposed by the state, which educates its citizens and conducts its official business in a particular tongue. And third, people typically identify much more closely with their native language than they do with their word processing program. These differences may explain why people are more humiliated by global English.

While the first two differences – the difficulty of switching languages, and the state's imposition of an official idiom – are important, I doubt that they explain the insult in global English. The parity of esteem complaint is meant to arise even in a situation where non-Anglophones have already learned English and been fairly compensated for their investment in accordance with appropriate principles of cooperative justice. The idea is that there is an *additional* injustice – beyond any unfair distribution of burdens or costs – in using English, because this use insults the speakers of other languages. But the explanation of this additional injustice cannot refer back to an unfair distribution of burdens, since *ex hypothesi*, that unfairness has already been taken care of. The second difference – that languages are often imposed by the state – cannot explain the insult in global English either. It is the microchoices of private individuals, not official public policies, that are driving the use of English in transnational contexts. Since states are not currently in the business of mandating global languages, there is no complaint about the 'non-neutrality' of state policies here.[1]

What about the third difference? Perhaps it is the fact that people care greatly about their native language, and feel very strongly identified with it, that explains the humiliation they perceive in global English? Certainly, this seems closer to the mark. Still, I doubt that people's subjective identification – by itself – can explain the threat to their equal dignity. For people also care very strongly about many things besides language. Yet only sometimes is it reasonable to feel humiliated when social institutions make it more difficult for me to pursue projects with which I strongly identify. Consider another area in which we have strong incentives to converge on a common social standard: the public workday. Shared social norms about working hours, like shared social norms about language, can make it difficult to pursue my projects and values. It is harder for me to indulge my passion for, say, organic farming, when I have to do all my teaching between the hours of 9 am and 5 pm. It would be better for me if Princeton University accommodated my preferences for scheduling work and leisure time, allowing me to farm all day and teach my students only at night. But surely the fact that my projects are disadvantaged by the public workday, in comparison with some conceivable alternative, is not sufficient to say my dignity – or the dignity of my community of organic farmers! – has been insulted here. To hold otherwise would allow that my dignity is insulted whenever I do not get what I strongly want. And surely that opens the door to all kinds of unreasonable 'dignity-based' demands. So why isn't the convergence on English as a global lingua franca the same? Why invoke the more morally serious complaint of a failure of equal respect?

No doubt many readers will find this analogy between our linguistic and our occupational preferences somewhat fanciful. It might be argued that, unlike our occupation, our native language structures our very memories and thoughts, giving it an especially close connection to personal identity. Still, I doubt that identification, on its own, allows us to successfully distinguish reasonable from unreasonable 'parity of esteem' complaints. For it is undeniable that people are strongly identified with a very wide range of things. Some people *do* identify with their occupational or recreational pursuits more strongly than with their language. Yet if the fact of subjective identification is sufficient to show that a social standard insults one's dignity, then we are committed to accommodating a kaleidoscopic multiplicity of identity-based claims. If we wish to avoid that conclusion, then some further criterion, by which we might distinguish reasonable from unreasonable feelings of insult, seems required. I'm not sure that Van Parijs has offered us such a criterion. But I do share his intuition that there is a greater problem with global English than with the choice of Word over Word Perfect, or daytime over nighttime working hours.

My main aim here was to highlight the need for some criterion by which to distinguish reasonable from unreasonable dignity-based complaints. But, as a tentative proposal, let me explore one idea that seems to me promising in this area. We might explain the threat to dignity by reference to the background power inequalities against which individual language learning-decisions take place. These background facts include the global military, economic, and political hegemony of Anglophone countries, and especially the United States. These countries are among the wealthiest in the world, making them dominant in international trade and foreign investment; their universities enjoy ascendancy in global higher education, which makes learning English a necessary means to acquisition of advanced knowledge; Anglophone countries exercise predominant control in international institutions, giving English a privileged status in the operations of these institutions; and English-language movies, TV shows, books, and other programming are diffused everywhere, a fact which imprints Anglophone tastes and values on the entire modern world. All these factors make it especially rational for people to choose English as a second language, because only *English* will grant them access to the global centers of political, economic, military, and cultural power. It is not as if a random cascade had suddenly shifted people's language-learning habits in favor of, say, Zulu, in the aftermath of which it became rational for others to adopt Zulu as well. Rather, English *is* the salient choice as a global lingua franca only because of the prior paramountcy of English-speaking states, and by extension, of their citizens.

When people use English in transnational contexts, then, they are indeed 'bowing' to the dominance of Anglophone countries in a real sense. Had it not been for those countries' hegemony, we would never have converged on English as our global lingua franca in the first place. To me, that is why it seems reasonable for non-Anglophones to feel insulted by the dominance of English. Had *some other* country attained international preeminence, it might have been *their* native language we would all be using. Global English, on this view, is just one more privilege that accrues to the inhabitants of Anglophone states, along with their wealth, their business and political connections, their power to unilaterally sanction other countries from whose policies they dissent, and their unequal access to visas that allow them to travel anywhere in the world they might wish to go.

If this is right, it suggests a more general criterion by which we might evaluate the reasonableness of 'dignity-based' complaints. It is reasonable to feel insulted by the choice of a social standard that diverges from one's preferences where background power inequalities between groups have caused that social standard to be structured in the way it is. This might occur because a more powerful group has used the lever of the state to impose its sectarian preferences on others, or, more subtly, because prior facts about its dominance systematically structured individuals' private choices in ways that reinforce that dominance. In such cases, one's dignity is indeed insulted by the requirement of conformity with these social norms. But in cases where background power relations between socially salient groups played no role in structuring prevailing standards – as in the choice of Word over Word Perfect, or the 9 am–5 pm workday – then it is not reasonable to invoke the 'parity of esteem' objection.[2]

Even where a legitimate parity of esteem complaint exists, that reason will not always be dispositive. Parity of esteem reasons need to be weighed against countervailing considerations, like coordination, administrative costs, other people's legitimate expectations, and so on. So there will be some cases in which – though a group's dignity is indeed insulted by a prevailing social standard – we should not reconfigure that standard, since the cost would be too great. But parity of esteem does give us an important *pro tanto* reason to reconfigure our institutions, and one that can justify the imposition of at least moderate costs. Even where a parity of esteem complaint cannot be fully accommodated, moreover, it still generates duties: for example, we ought to offer a justification that shows why important public purposes cannot reasonably be achieved without this particular disadvantage. This justification requirement is important, since it demonstrates our shared commitment to the equal dignity of socially salient groups. Unlike subjective identification, then, I believe that the background power inequality criterion may allow us to more successfully distinguish between reasonable and unreasonable complaints. And whether or not my particular proposal for making this distinction succeeds, I believe some such criterion is certainly needed.

Setting aside my proposal about how best to interpret the 'parity of esteem' complaint, I now want to ask whether Van Parijs's solution – the linguistic territoriality principle – is a successful response to it. The linguistic territoriality principle holds that each language community should be granted the right to impose its own language as the medium of public administration, political participation and education within a territory. The community must be willing to bear the costs associated with protecting its language, by extending access to an adequate level of proficiency to all permanent residents, and by accepting whatever reduction in economic competitiveness its policy might entail. According to Van Parijs, this territoriality principle helps to prevent the development of a 'colonial' attitude on the part of speakers of more widespread languages, such as English. Outsiders settling on the territory will be required to learn and educate their children in the official language of this particular place, thereby 'bowing' to a weaker tongue's ascendancy. The territorial regime also prevents the maxi-min dynamics from permanently eroding weaker languages to the point of extinction. Finally, it allows each language to become the 'queen' of a political unit (though not necessarily a fully sovereign one) somewhere on the globe.

Perhaps surprisingly, then, Van Parijs's cosmopolitan egalitarianism ends up partly endorsing the nationalist principle that political units should be congruent with cultural ones, and specifically with linguistic groups (Gellner 1983, p. 1, see also Miller 1995, pp. 81–118). Of course, Van Parijs makes space for nationalism only up to a point, since he also supports the parallel development of supranational political institutions. But, for him, linguistic communities have the right to claim political autonomy within a territory in order to protect and preserve their languages.

Does this linguistic territoriality principle achieve its intended goal, of securing the equal dignity of individuals who speak different languages? Here I am skeptical. As Van Parijs himself notes, a difficult challenge for the view is the fact of linguistic heterogeneity. To claim that the territoriality principle adequately secures parity of esteem, we need to picture the world as neatly divided into distinct linguistic communities, each of which maps readily onto a separate geographical area. But this is false: territories everywhere are inhabited by a linguistically diverse mix of people, including immigrants, refugees, and national or indigenous minorities (De Schutter 2008, pp. 110–111). Once this linguistic heterogeneity is factored in, doesn't a territorial solution simply replicate the worrisome colonialist dynamic it was designed to prevent? When some residents of the territory do not belong to the preferred linguistic community, aren't these people slighted by being made to 'bow' to the official language, forced to adopt it in their transactions with the state, to school their children in it, and to use it when they enter the public sphere?

Van Parijs considers several possible responses to the heterogeneity problem. One possibility – quite plausible, it seems to me – would be to require that linguistically heterogeneous territories be officially multilingual, on grounds that this is more consistent with parity of esteem. But Van Parijs largely dismisses the multilingual approach. He considers two variants of it. On a *disjunctive multilingual approach*, the regime offers citizens the choice of educating their children and communicating with the state in whichever of the many languages within the territory they prefer. Van Parijs finds this approach inadequate because it does nothing to prevent the stronger language from driving out the weaker language(s) over time, as maxi-min dynamics between diverse speakers begin to take hold. Even if the state provides services in a weaker language, the stronger one may still dominate when it comes to people's everyday interactions. So a *disjunctive approach* does not provide sufficient guarantees for linguistic survival. If, on the other hand, the political regime pursues a *conjunctive approach*, requiring all its citizens to learn all the officially recognized languages, then this quickly imposes an upper bound on the number of languages that can be recognized and is very demanding in terms of expenditure and effort. Van Parijs believes it will hardly ever work in practice.

So for the most part, Van Parijs reacts to the problem of linguistic hetero-geneity not by recommending official multilingualism, but rather by counseling further territorial subdivision. He favors chopping territories into unilingual zones that can maximize the inclusion of native speakers of the recognized lan-guage and minimize the inclusion of non-native speakers. Political units should, as much as possible, be gerrymandered around language groups (p. 166).

Yet this 'territorial subdivision' solution simply re-confronts the original problem. Unless people can easily move or be moved, any continuous geo-graphical space will always include some people who do not belong to the pre-vailing linguistic community, no matter how small we draw the units. What are we to do about those linguistic minorities who remain 'trapped?' Van Parijs offers us only a very limited response. He claims that it is appropriate to intro-duce transitional accommodations for 'trapped' allophones at the moment new borders are introduced. Non-native speakers alive when boundaries are redrawn who find their ability to live in their own language jeopardized, can demand some temporary continuation of the services they previously enjoyed. They can keep using their minority language in communications with the state, and (for a time) schooling their children in it. But eventually these transitional measures will end: any people born after the cutoff date will be educated in the official territorial language. Thus, future generations of allophones will be required – eventually – to accept the elimination of their language's public use on that territory.

Is this outcome acceptable, if what we care about is parity of esteem? What we can we say to the linguistic minority member, to convince her that she enjoys equal respect here? One thing we might say is that the system produces a kind of 'reciprocity' at the global level: the minority member's language may well be protected in some other place. If she lived there, then she would be entitled to expect immigrants and minorities on the territory to 'bow' to her native tongue's dominance (p. 149). So perhaps she should accept that turn-about is fair play, and be willing to 'bow' to the dominant language in the territory where she now resides.

Yet how is it supposed to bolster the dignity of this particular person to know that her language might be a 'queen' on some other territory? As I understand the parity of esteem complaint, it is not a complaint that *languages* are treated unequally across the globe. It is rather a complaint that *people* are treated unequally, by being continually required to accommodate to a more powerful group in their everyday interactions, in a way that reinforces their subordinate status. *This* indignity is not at all expunged by the knowledge that if one lived somewhere else, one would be one of the favored inhabitants in that other place. For one is still subordinate in *this* place, here and now.

Perhaps we can say to the trapped minority member that if she really wishes to speak her language in public – and to see her children grow up in it – she can always move. Would that be an adequate response? If resettlement is sufficiently easy, maybe it would. If she merely has to relocate ten miles down the road, then that is probably an acceptable price to pay. Moving ten miles is unlikely to disrupt her personal and family ties, and she can probably keep working at her current job and participating in most of the social practices that matter to her. But since a person's family, friends, workplace, cultural, and associative bonds – the whole structure of her life – are usually located in her territory of permanent residence, it is not a reasonable response to require her to uproot herself and relocate to some very distant area. For that means that she has to give up almost everything else that matters to her in order to secure parity of esteem.

Thinking about what we might say to the trapped minority member, then, highlights a serious problem with the strategy of pursuing parity of esteem by means of a linguistic territoriality principle. This principle simply replicates the very 'colonialist' dynamics of domination and subordination it was designed to mitigate, by conferring special privileges on one linguistic group at the expense of others within a territory. Allowing the preferred group's language to 'own' the public space devalues citizens from other linguistic backgrounds, consigning them to second-class status within the area. But we cannot actually secure parity of esteem in this way. Conferring special preferences only reinforces the dynamics of power and subordination that drives the 'parity of esteem' complaint in the first place.

So is there a better way? I believe that official multilingualism provides a superior approach to managing linguistic heterogeneity. While I cannot elaborate a full institutional proposal here, let me simply describe three multilingual regimes that have been outlined elsewhere in the literature. Any one of these regimes, I think, would provide a better way of securing parity of esteem than the linguistic territoriality principle. The first variant, *official multilingualism*, holds that all the different languages spoken in a territory can claim equivalent public support. Equal public services should be provided in each language spoken, no matter how many speakers that language has. The main objection to this model is that it would be costly and cumbersome, and provokes potentially wasteful state expenditure. On the second variant, *prorated official multilingualism*, some account is taken of the number of speakers demanding services in a recognized language, so that the state must provide the same *per capita* level of assistance to each group. This may mean that languages with smaller numbers of speakers receive fewer services, or have to travel farther to access these services (Patten 2003). This responds to the concern about wasteful expenditure, by limiting language assistance to the fair claims of that community of speakers on public resources. The third variant, the *least cost model*, accepts that states have reason to impose some rationalization in a common language, where that rationalization serves compelling public purposes – for example, in access to economic opportunity or democratic participation. Still, these reasons for imposing a language must be balanced against an equally important reason to acknowledge the equal standing of linguistic minorities.

On balance, then, states should *narrowly tailor* their rationalization policies, by granting these linguistic minorities the right to publicly promote their languages (e.g. through bilingual schooling) alongside the common language (Stilz 2009).

I believe that any of these multilingual regimes would allow the polity to more credibly claim to secure parity of esteem than the linguistic territoriality principle. Under that principle, the polity sends the message that the majority linguistic group 'owns' the territory and its political institutions and that minorities have only second-class status. Yet surely this is problematic: the polity's commitment to parity of esteem ought to be publicly reflected in its political institutions, in the justifications that are offered for various language policies, in the way citizens treat one another, and the attitudes and expectations they have of those who are not members of the majority linguistic group. Only a multilingual regime can secure this important public goal of acknowledging equal standing under conditions of linguistic heterogeneity.

Let me conclude, then, by considering thee objections that one might make to such a multilingual regime. First, one might object that it is simply impossible for the state to be 'neutral' with respect to language (Kymlicka 1995, pp. 110–111). So why should we try to achieve the impossible? I think this objection misfires. It is true that the state cannot ensure *equal success* for all the languages on its territory. Yet the state can establish a language policy that treats speakers of different languages fairly, by not specially privileging one linguistic group over others. It can do this by recognizing multiple languages, providing some public support to all these languages, and offering a justification for any imposed rationalization in a common language that references a genuinely compelling public purpose that cannot be pursued in any less restrictive way.

Second, it might be objected that a multilingual regime cannot adequately ensure language survival. Van Parijs argues that once a linguistically diverse group of people interact with one another, the maxi-min dynamics will take hold, and more powerful languages will tend to drive out the weaker ones (pp. 143–145). I would respond, however, by questioning whether parity of esteem actually requires language survival. If, against a set of rules that publicly express the state's commitment to the equal standing of different linguistic groups, some people decide to assimilate to a different language, I do not see any injustice in the loss. The commitment to parity of esteem, again, is a commitment to the equal dignity of *individuals*, not the equal dignity of *languages*. It might be objected here that an individual can only freely decide to abandon his or her language under fair background conditions. But once the maxi-min dynamics are in play, some individuals may lack the genuine option of continuing to speak their native tongue. In response, I make two points. First, it seems prematurely pessimistic to believe that minority languages will always be driven out in a multilingual context. Under a multilingual regime, the state does a great deal to support individuals' ability to continue speaking their native languages, by providing them significant education and public services in those languages. Second, even if some languages struggle under these conditions, it is not always unfair to face background conditions that preclude one's projects flourishing to the degree that one desires. Citizens do not have a right against the state that all their projects succeed, but only that the state treats them fairly and even-handedly, balancing their claims against the equivalent claims of others with different projects. If the state does institute fair background rules, and still some languages do not succeed, this may be regrettable, but it is not an injustice (see Patten 2014 for a similar argument).

Finally, we might object, as Van Parijs does, that a multilingual regime risks walling off citizens into distinct and mutually unintelligible enclaves, thereby posing a threat to social cohesion (p. 148, 196). But this depends significantly on which model of multilingualism we adopt. Both *pro-rated multilingualism* and *the least cost model* can accept that in certain cases, there are compelling reasons for promoting a common public language. But they deny that these reasons suffice to justify aiming at linguistic homogeneity, and these views point out that there are important countervailing reasons for the state to publicly demonstrate its commitment to the equality of linguistic minorities. We might plausibly think that the balance of these two reasons requires us to leave significant space for the public support of minority languages.

To sum up, then, while Van Parijs has convincingly argued for an additional dimension of justice he calls 'parity of esteem', he has not fully explained why the global dominance of English poses a threat to equal esteem, nor why the linguistic territoriality principle is the right response. I believe English threatens the dignity of speakers of other languages only because background power inequalities are in large part driving its adoption. And I have argued that Van Parijs's linguistic territoriality principle does not provide the right response to our parity of esteem concerns. Under conditions of linguistic heterogeneity, only a multilingual regime can succeed at addressing these important issues. Allowing majority groups to claim hegemony within a territory, on the other hand, only incentivizes conflict and subordination. And that is not the kind of respectful transnational cooperation that we want as a basis for a future global *demos*.

Acknowledgments
I would like to thank Helder De Schutter, Philippe Van Parijs, and an anonymous reviewer for helpful comments on this paper.

Disclosure statement
No potential conflict of interest was reported by the author.

Notes

1. One might object that though there is no state-imposed global language, international institutions such as the EU, IMF, World Bank, or the aviation sector privilege English, and this structures individuals' learning choices. I agree that this fact is significant, and discuss it further below.

2. One might hold that even without background power inequalities, the fact that a particular group's language is chosen as a *lingua franca* is sufficient to single out that group for higher status. But I doubt this. In the nineteenth century, for example, French was the language of international diplomacy, though the French were not economically or politically superior to the other Great Powers. Did the mere use of the French language at international conferences give the French a publicly superior status *vis à vis* the British, Germans, or Americans?

Notes on contributor

Anna Stilz is associate professor of politics at Princeton University. Her first book, Liberal Loyalty: Freedom, Obligation, and the State, was published by Princeton University Press in 2009. She has also published articles in Ethics, History of European Ideas, International Theory, Journal of Political Philosophy, Philosophy and Public Affairs, and Policy and Society.

References

De Schutter, H., 2008. The linguistic territoriality principle – a critique. *Journal of applied philosophy*, 25 (2), 105–120.

Gellner, E., 1983. *Nations and nationalism*. Ithaca: Cornell.

Kymlicka, W., 1995. *Multicultural citizenship*. Oxford: Oxford University Press.

Miller, D., 1995. *On nationality*. Oxford: Oxford University Press.

Patten, A., 2003. Liberal neutrality and language policy. *Philosophy and public affairs*, 31 (4), 356–386.

Patten, A., 2014. *Equal recognition: the moral foundations of minority rights*. Princeton, NJ: Princeton University Press.

Stilz, A., 2009. Civic nationalism and language policy. *Philosophy and public affairs*, 37 (3), 257–292.

Van Parijs, P., 1995. *Real freedom for all: what, if anything, can justify capitalism?* Oxford: Oxford University Press.

Van Parijs, P., 2007. International distributive justice. *In*: R. Goodin, P. Pettit, and T. Pogge, eds. *A companion to contemporary political philosophy*. Oxford: Blackwell, 437–473.

Van Parijs, P., 2011. *Linguistic justice for Europe and for the world*. Oxford: Oxford University Press.

One-way conversation with Philippe Van Parijs

Jean Laponce

Department of Political Science, University of British Columbia, Vancouver, BC, Canada

This essay reacts to Philippe Van Parijs's arguments in favor of English as the global lingua franca and in favor of the territorial protection of the languages of minority nations. I agree with both arguments. But I see the case for the lingua franca as a matter of convenience rather than justice. And I don't link territorial protection to the emergence of English, but instead ground it as a fundamental right of national self-determination.

This essay on Van Parijs's *Linguistic Justice for Europe and for the World* (2011) takes the form of a one-way conversation with the author concerning his two major public policy recommendations: Helping rather than objecting to the surge of English as the world lingua franca (notably as L2) and protecting native languages (L1) by giving the political authority of the area of concentration of the L1 coercive power over language use in the public domain (official language, language of instruction, language of contracts for example). I shall weave that conversation around two reactions: Yes and But.

Yes

Yes, I agree that the spread of a lingua franca within Europe and through the world should not only be welcomed but should be helped. Philippe Van Parijs reaches that conclusion on the premise that communication through a single world language would be beneficial to all since it would reduce the cost of communication (no need to rely on interpreters) and is morally commendable since it would satisfy Montaigne's hope that nothing human should remain foreign to us.

But

I too realize that English is, at present, the only lingua franca capable of covering the globe. But, for how long? Lingua francas come and go. If Van Parijs and Laponce were suddenly projected a mere 150 years back, to a time when

Rivarol was reflecting on the reasons for the universality of French, we would both have ignored English and sided for French and, if we pursue the mind experiment by projecting us 150 years into the future, we would probably agree that we do not know.[1]

Another small **but** occurs to me: Is it so obvious that increasing the amount of communication among humans is beneficial to all? It is said that when Newton was offered to become a member of the Royal Society he hesitated and said "Is that not likely to increase dangerously the number of my acquaintances?". As things stand, I often feel that, though I guard against communication overload, I nevertheless suffer from it. Under a single world-wide lingua franca, how much greater the overload for someone out there on the margins of an English speaking world who has to converse and write in an unfamiliar language. Would not that individual think, more than occasionally, of the good old days as those when language and relevant community had roughly the same boundaries? I thus wonder whether Philippe Van Parijs's taking the desired goal of a lingua franca to be the ability of two humans, taken at random the world over, to speak to each other in a common language, is a measure of success or a cause for regret. Probably both, but in much varying proportions according to time, nation, and profession (I shall have to come back later to what I mean by nation).

Having a lingua franca as a native language or acquiring it as an L2 has likely noticeable effects on social stratification. English as well as French have well served both PVP and Laponce and many others, both academically and socially and that may have distorted the hierarchy of merit and competence. If distortion there is when the lingua franca is not universal that distortion should disappear if the lingua franca becomes universal except that any lingua franca would distinguish those who know it well from those who do not. An assumption of equality does not meet the problem. If one presumes, as I do, that inequality is the norm, one cannot avoid facing the fact that lingua francas impact the social hierarchy. To do so may I, like Van Parijs, use a personal recollection? It concerns language and hierarchy in the *International Political Science Association* in the 1980s. That association's official languages were and still are French and English, but its governing language has in fact become restricted to English following the enlargement of the membership to a greater number of national associations. The evolution was similar to that described by Van Parijs in the case of the European Union. As the number of native languages increased, the use of French diminished and that of English grew. But, among speakers of English, the hierarchy of knowledge and the ability to be easily understood became more obvious. Acquiring a universal lingua franca, acquiring it more or less, has not only some equalizing effects in facilitating communication, it is also a source of cleavage according to the level of knowledge, and the ability to communicate in that language between have and have not, between have and have to lesser degrees. My unquantified experience, in academic settings at least, is that a too accented English may disqualify from office.

Yes

Yes, I fully agree: a minority language is best protected by coercive territorial authorities of its own. Speakers of a particular language need and prefer to congregate in space in order to speak with and understand their grocers, teachers, doctors, clergy, friends, and family. Even in the age of easy and rapid communication, the friction of physical space on communication is still considerable in terms of delay and distortion.

And **yes,** I agree also that not all languages are necessarily to be protected. Some are prisons from which speakers would not mind and may actually want to escape (against the wish of some anthropologists who would prefer re-instilling ethnic fervor rather than offering emancipation). Van Parijs says that he does not propose to give all languages a right of protection but does not set criteria of exclusion. I propose two major conditions to their political protection: (a) the likelihood that the authorities of the protected linguistic community be of good international citizenship (b) approval by that community.

The first condition (a) is unavoidably cast in very vague terms. It would include democratic societies but not only those. I shall not deal with that condition here beyond saying that the restriction is intended to avoid supporting rogue, corrupt or tyrannical authorities with powers over education and the language of public institutions.

But

But my second condition (b) raises the difficult issue of boundaries, a major ethical issue that requires practical solutions. If a people speaking a language X is set within a sovereign state where the dominant language Y is that of most citizens, the geographical contact between the two languages is unlikely to separate X and Y very neatly; but even if it does, an exceptional case, the boundary of the language to be protected still poses a problem unless we can ascertain how many speakers of X want to have their language protected by a coercive authority of their own. It may also be that valuing language varies across the territory concerned and that setting a boundary on the basis of the so-called objective criteria such as censuses would be against the wishes of at least some and possibly many individuals caught within the 'objective' boundary. Furthermore, when the contact between languages is through zones of mixed settlements, a frequent case, it is increasingly hazardous to assume that the census type of geographical distribution of minority and majority languages will lead to proper boundaries. Consulting the populations concerned by referendum is an imperative. Philippe Van Parijs deals with the use of the referendum but in the sole context of the relations between center and units of a federal multilingual society, notably Belgium and Switzerland (p. 149 and p. 263, note 27). I would have preferred an expanded coverage to include the use of the referendum for either splitting territorially or keeping together minority and dominant languages of an existing state. But first, I need to specify what I mean by *nation* before showing how I come to conclusions similar to those of Philippe Van Parijs through an entirely different route.

The term *nation* is particularly ambiguous in English since it is used to refer to sovereign states (as in *United Nations),* to a government speaking for a particular state (as in International Relations), to the people of a given state or ethnic or religion or political unit of a federation (as when the Canadian Government recognizes Quebec as a nation) or to only part of Quebec (as when the *Parti québécois* refers to its separatist supporters). The context suffices usually to clarify the meaning. Van Parijs takes it to refer to sovereign states and their linguistic and regional components within their existing boundaries, notably Belgium and Switzerland. He thus avoids the problem of resetting international as well as internal boundaries. By contrast, starting with the understanding of the nation as a community of people having or wanting to have the political control of their destinies, one is led to consider the role of inter- as well as intra-states boundaries and referendums.

I begin my own argument in favor of national self-determination and referendum, as does Renan (1882), with the premise that nations have the right to govern themselves either independently or, if they prefer, autonomously within a larger polity. By right I do not mean a legally enforceable right but a moral, an ethical right subject only to the restrictions of viability and good citizenship already mentioned.[2]

If the right of self-determination is made operational, internally or internationally, the problem of boundaries is likely to occur; but it took more than a century of sovereignty referendums (from 1791 to 1920) to accept that democratic principles required that a referendum area could be split, if needed, by a territorial boundary (one boundary to simplify the demonstration). The first recorded referendum of sovereignty, that of Avignon in 1791, was approved by a majority of voters in Avignon itself but not in its rural attachment of the Comtat Venaissin that would have preferred remaining under the authority of the Pope. It was wrongly assumed that the decision had to be made by the voters as a single unit. Prior to the transfer of sovereignty of Savoy from Piemont to France in 1860, there was some discussion of a possible transfer of some part of Savoie to Switzerland to satisfy the local residents, but there again the referendum transferred the whole territory to France. The democratic breakthrough came only in 1919 when the Paris Peace Conference adopted the Wilson principles of self-determination to give minority nations from Germany, Austria, and Hungary (in Schleswig, Allenstein, Marienwerder, Klagenfurt, Sopron, and Upper Silesia) the option of separating and by so doing protecting more effectively their culture and language.

Let us take Schleswig as an example. The referendum area was divided into two zones that voted separately. In the first zone, that closest to Denmark, 74% of the voters favored joining Denmark. In the second zone, closer to Germany, 79% voted to remain part of Germany. On the basis of the figures given by Wambaugh (1933), I estimate that this innovative procedure raised the level of popular satisfaction to 73%, far better than 53% if there had been a single voting area and a single deciding count (Laponce 2012, p. 124).

A further progress was made by Switzerland, when Jura separated from Bern. Admittedly, the long procedure (voting was spread over more than a year and three successive ballots) required strong democratic nerves and commitment, but offers a marked improvement over the 50% + 1 typically used by simply counting the votes of individuals irrespective of their area of residence, hence failing to distinguish a territorially concentrated minority wishing its autonomy or independence from a larger dominant group.

The issue, pressed by Jura separatists in 1974, was whether the Francophone Jura should separate from Bern and become a canton of its own within the Swiss federation (McRae 1983, Jenkins 1987, Laponce 2010, 2012).[3]

The first ballot asked all citizens of the Jura whether a Jura canton should be created. The vote of 50.7% in favor decided that a new canton of Jura would be instituted but no boundary was set at that point.

A second ballot, held eight months later, was restricted to the regions of the Jura that had voted against the creation of the new canton. Each of those regions could request by a petition signed by at least 1/5th of their electors that a regional referendum be held to decide whether the region would join the Jura in the making or remain part of Bern. The three regions that had initially voted against the secession from Bern requested a referendum which confirmed their preference to stay within Bern.

The third and last referendum was made available, through a petition similar to that of the second ballot, to the communes (the smallest unit of local government) lying on either side of the tentative boundary resulting from the first two referendums. Eight communes shifted from Bern to Jura while two made the opposite choice. That last vote determined the new boundary separating Jura from Bern.

The case of the Jura illustrates, firstly, how wrong one would be if one failed to consult by referendum the populations whose language one wants to protect and relied instead on the boundaries suggested by the so-called 'objective' sources such as censuses. And it shows, secondly, that one can, through successive referendums, obtain the convergence of liberal and communitarian democracy. Hence, the wish that Van Parijs would give more attention to territorial split of existing states and the use of the sovereignty referendum to solve or at least reduce internal language conflicts.[4]

Yes

Is linguistic diversity a good thing? The hyper diversity of many African countries is a major obstacle to economic progress and to political stability. The manageable and well-managed diversity of Switzerland is a model. Diversity has become a buzz word of contemporary politics that fails to distinguish linguistic diversity by superposition from diversity by juxtaposition.[5] The germanophone Swiss, who speaks Standard German; Swiss German, French, and English, and sometimes Italian as well, is no exception. Yet favoring such high superposition of languages at the individual level does not prevent Switzerland from having one of the more effective and stringent territorial grounding of its official languages. The Germanophone from the city of Bern who crosses the language boundary into francophone Bern and settles there will be able to continue using his German or Italian or any other language of his or her choice in private but will have to use French in the public domain: schools or contracts for example. I fully agree with Van Parijs that favoring individual multilingualism is not in contradiction with the enforcement of unilingualism in the public domain within the properly selected boundaries of a public authority established to protect the minority.

Yes and But to conclude

My two conclusions are the same as those of Van Parijs, but mine are not linked. I say *yes* to not only welcoming but also pushing for the further growth of English as the world lingua franca and *yes* to the territorial protection of minority nations who want to protect their language by means of coercive political authorities of their own, notably by establishing the minority language as sole official language and sole language of education (except of course for the teaching of foreign tongues). But I do not link these two conclusions through the notion of justice. I see the world dominance of English as a convenience in a globalizing world (notably in trade and science) but do not expect that this will equalize conditions as much as contributing to the strengthening of social hierarchies in favor of leaders speaking fluent English.

As for the protection of minority languages, I do not link it to what is done to one or more lingua francas. I simply deduct it from the fundamental human right of nations to self-determination. I thus do not see the need for parity of esteem that is a key to Van Parijs's demonstration. That there be such esteem is obviously desirable but not necessary. However, to conclude, the essential is that our two different approaches lead us to similar policy recommendations.

Disclosure statement
No potential conflict of interest was reported by the author.

Notes
1. Considering only the languages spoken worldwide by more than a million people and narrowing the catch by requiring that the language be L1 in at least 40 countries, one obtains the following hierarchy based on the latest statistics of *Ethnologue:* English 112 countries, French 60, Arabic 57, Spanish 44, German 43. The same languages ranked by the number of their L1 speakers (in millions) are of

course markedly different: Chinese 1213, Spanish 329, English 328, Arabic 221, German 90, French 67. See <*ethnologue.com/ethno.docs/distribution.asp?by=size*>. consulted 6 September 2012.

2. Renan (1882), who rightly denies that either race, language, economic interests, religion, geography, or military considerations be valid definers of a nation, is within the tradition of the French revolutionists of the 1790s who justified the transfer of sovereignty of Avignon from the Holy See to France on the sole ground that this was the wish of the people, and wrote in the constitution of 1791 that a people's right of self-determination was fundamental and inalienable. The Charter of the United Nations says roughly the same but the provision was interpreted to apply only to colonies and the politics of the Cold War led to interpret the right of self-determination to mean, for polities other than colonies, the right to choose their type of internal regime. That interpretation was backed by the so-called *territorial contract* and the *uti possidetis juris* principle that have been rendered largely obsolete by the end of the Cold War. Since then, international doctrine as well as practice have partly moved back to the views of the French Revolution, of Renan and of Woodrow Wilson. See Buchanan (1997); Ghebrewebet (2006); Laponce (2010, pp. 156–160); (Sebastian *et al.* (2010).

3. The language boundary that separated and still separates francophone from germanophone areas of Switzerland coincides with some cantonal boundaries but not with all. The canton of Bern was in 1974 and still is today divided by an official language boundary which was not an issue in the referendum.

4. The germanophone district of Laufen, separated by the secession of Jura from the germanophone part of Bern, decided to join the nearby Germanophone canton of Basel-country.

5. The concept of diversity often fails to distinguish the consequences of either mixing or separating. If we shake yellow, blue, green, and red pieces of paper within a glass container, we change the overall composition of the display while retaining each of the original colors; but if we mix paints of yellow, blue, green, and red on our palette, we create uniformity.

Notes on contributor

Jean Laponce is professor emeritus of Political Science at the University of British Columbia, Canada. He published more than 120 articles and many books on languages, minority rights, federalism, self-determination, and nationalism, including *Languages and Territories* (1987), *The Protection of Minorities* (1961), *Loi de Babel et autres régularités des rapports entre langue et politique* (2006), *Le referendum de souveraineté* (2010).

References

Buchanan, A., 1997. Theories of secession. *Philosophy and public affairs*, 26, 31–61.
Ethnologue, 2012. Dallas Institute of Linguistics. Available from: www.sil.ethnologue
Ghebrewebet, H., 2006. *Identifying units of statehood and determining international boundaries: a revised look at the doctrine of uti possidetis and the principle of self-determination*. Bern: Verlag Peter Lang.
Jenkins, J., 1987. French speaking Switzerland and the Jura problem. *In*: J. Jenkins, ed. *Indigenous minority groups in multinational democracies in the year 2000: problems and prospects*. Waterloo: Wilfred Laurier University Press, 208 p.

Laponce, J., 2010. *Le référendum de souveraineté: comparaisons, critiques et commentaires* [The sovereignty referendum: comparisons, criticisms, and commentaries]. Québec: Presses de l'Université Laval.

Laponce, J., 2012. Language and sovereignty referendums: the convergence effect. *Nationalism and ethnic politics*, 18, 113–128.

McRae, K., 1983. *Conflict and compromise in multilingual societies: Switzerland.* Waterloo: Wilfrid Laurier University Press.

Renan, E., 1882. *Qu'est-ce qu'une nation et autres écrits politiques* [What is a nation and other political writings]. Paris: Imprimerie nationale.

Sebastian, C., Anstis St., J., and Zacher, M., 2010. The normative bases of the global territorial order. *Diplomacy and statecraft*, 21, 306–321.

Van Parijs, P., 2011. *Linguistic justice for Europe and for the world.* Oxford: Oxford University Press.

Wambaugh, S., 1933. *Plebiscites since the world war.* Washington: Carnegie Endowment for International Peace.

Can parity of self-esteem serve as the basis of the principle of linguistic territoriality?

Daniel Weinstock

Faculty of Law, McGill University, Montreal, Canada

In this paper, I argue that Philippe Van Parijs' argument for the principle of linguistic territoriality rests upon an unexamined and unvindicated assumption, to the effect that most situations in which smaller languages are threatened by larger ones can be assimilated to 'colonial cases', that is to cases in which there is injustice as between the two linguistic groups, as opposed to 'mere number cases', that is cases in which linguistic groups of different sizes coexist in the absence of injustice. Moreover, I argue that Van Parijs underestimates the amount of coercion that will have to be applied even within linguistically defined territories in order to avoid the erosion of the smaller language.

Introduction

Philippe Van Parijs' *Linguistic Justice for Europe and for the World* makes two main claims. The first is that it is a good thing that a *lingua franca* is emerging in the world today. A global *lingua franca* is required for the creation of a trans-national *demos*, which is itself a requirement of egalitarian justice (Van Parijs 2011, p. 28). That the global *lingua franca* is *English* (rather than, say, an artificial language at equal linguistic distance from natural languages) poses problems of distributive justice. Native speakers of other languages must make investments in order to learn the emerging *lingua franca* that native English-speakers do not have to make. But Van Parijs argues that the overcoming of this asymmetry does not require the setting up of complex mechanisms of redistribution. The ubiquity of English is in a sense both the problem, and the source of a solution. While it imposes costs on others, it also provides speakers of other languages a way to meet those costs by allowing them the means to acquire the language cheaply.

The second major claim is that while the emergence of a global *lingua franca* is a good thing, global unlilingualism would be an unwelcome result.

Avoiding a tendency toward global unilingualism is however difficult because the same sociolinguistic mechanisms that lead to the emergence of a global *lingua franca* will over time tend to crowd out 'weaker' languages.[1] As English becomes ubiquitous, it will tend to be the language that speakers with different linguistic repertoires default to when they want to communicate with one another. Absent countervailing forces, English will become the de facto language of public interaction. This will tend to relegate other languages to private, more local settings. We would in this case be only one step from the folklorization, and ultimately, the disappearance of other languages.

Van Parijs argues that in order to avoid this drift, while preserving the advantages afforded by the existence of a *lingua franca*, the principle of linguistic territoriality (LT) must be adopted. Language groups should be able, to use Van Parijs' colorful expression, to 'grab a territory' and to enact coercive legislation on the territory they have staked out. Such coercive legislation, which would make it mandatory for all to learn and to make use of the local, 'weaker' language in public settings, offsets the drift toward unilingualism that the untrammeled operation of sociolinguistic processes favoring 'stronger' languages would put in place.

The obvious question, given Van Parijs' endorsement of the global *lingua franca* and of the normative grounds for its emergence, is why the trend toward unilingualism should be resisted. What values underpin the wish to arrest the sociolinguistic processes that lead to the spread of English at the point where that spread might become corrosive of other languages?

Note that Van Parijs does not believe that linguistic diversity is a good in and of itself (Van Parijs 2011, p. 206), nor does he believe that languages are the sources of valid moral claims above and beyond those of individuals. Van Parijs can therefore not argue that the drift toward unilingualism should be resisted because each language is intrinsically important, or because there is something intrinsically good about linguistic *diversity*. The argument defending the second claim must be couched in the language of (broadly) liberal justice, that is, in a theory of justice that is ultimately grounded in the valid moral claims of *individuals*.

Van Parijs believes that the principle of 'parity of self-esteem' can be invoked in this context. Acknowledging that considerations of self-esteem have not been given the importance they deserve in traditional theories of distributive justice (including the theory he himself developed in his earlier work), he argues that to allow the processes that are currently leading to the emergence of English as a global *lingua franca* to shade into a threat to weaker languages, and ultimately, to unilingualism, would be incompatible with the conditions for speakers of all languages to feel that they are of equal worth. Independently of considerations of equal opportunity, Van Parijs writes, '[i]n a just society, people must not be stigmatized, despised, disparaged, humiliated by virtue of their collective identity', where language is one of the vectors along which such identities develop (Van Parijs 2011).

In this paper I want to question Van Parijs' use of the 'equality of self-esteem' argument to ground the equilibrium that he wants to achieve. My claim will be, first, that his argument in *LJ* is premised upon a very specific kind of context in which pressures can come to be felt for the speakers of smaller languages to adopt the stronger language in a range of public settings. Call these 'colonial' contexts. I will be arguing that such contexts are not exhaustive of the range of cases in which sociolinguistic pressures toward unilingualism can come to be felt by speakers of weaker languages, and second, that in such contexts, what is at the basis of the justification of (otherwise illiberal) coercive legislation has to do not with deficits of self-esteem, but with the commission by others of injustices.

Second, I will hold that LT may not be sufficient to offset pressures toward unilingualism unless it engages in coercive legislation that falls foul of (broadly defined) liberal strictures on the use of state power. This is because while moderate constraints on language choice can have an impact on the extent of linguistic *competence* in the local language, much more draconian measures are required in order to affect language *use*.

Equality of self-esteem

In *A Theory of Justice*, Rawls lists 'self-respect (or self-esteem)' as 'perhaps the most important primary good' (Rawls 1971). Lack of self-respect undercuts the agent's ability to pursue his plan of life, and may also color the degree to which he views that plan of life as worth pursuing. The importance of self-respect thus resides in the fact that, where it is absent, no amount of the other primary goods will suffice to allow the agent to carry out his reasonable conception of the good life. Rawls lists two conditions as being particularly important to the attainment of self-respect. First, to quote Rawls, '[i]t normally suffices that for each person there is some association (one or more) to which he belongs and within which the activities that are rational for him are publicly affirmed by others' (Rawls 1971, p. 441). Second, self-respect is promoted when these associations exist within the context of fair background conditions of justice. Where all citizens share a public conception of justice that reflects their status as moral equals, associations will tend to be less inclined to compare themselves to others in order to acquire a sense of their worth. Where just background conditions of justice exist, the sources of excusable envy are absent.

The second condition that makes up Rawls' account of self-respect seems particularly important. Complex modern societies will unavoidably involve a great many inequalities. For example, people who have more esoteric plans of life may find that they face greater obstacles in carrying these plans out than will those whose plans are more popular. But in order for inequalities to generate *inequities*, those who experience deficits in self-respect have to be able to point to some aspect of the process that has produced the inequality of which it can truly be said that it does not treat them as moral equals. Were this condition not to be satisfied, then people's feelings of lack of self-esteem would be self-validating. For such feelings to ground legitimate moral claims, it is important that they reflect institutional shortfalls. Feelings, in and of themselves, do not constitute a principled basis upon which to determine whether certain citizens have been poorly treated in terms of their ability to access the 'social bases of self-respect'.

Extending Rawls' line of reasoning to the case of language groups, a first observation is that it would be a miracle were the world to divide up into language groups of equal 'strengths'. A variety of factors – geographic, sociological, etc. – can conspire to make it the case that certain languages are spoken by a greater number of people than others. All things equal, a wide range of circumstances make certain languages vulnerable to the kinds of sociolinguistic pressures that Van Parijs describes in his account of the rise of English to the status of *lingua franca*, and of the concomitant dangers posed to weaker languages.

Now, historically, it is certainly the case that the dominance of certain languages over others has been due not just to the mere coexistence within linguistic space of language groups of different sizes. Colonialism, for example, often had explicitly cultural and linguistic purposes. The goal was not just to plunder the resources of colonized peoples (though it was certainly that) but also to extinguish their languages and cultures not just through coercive measures aimed (for example) at prohibiting the teaching and use of native languages, but also through the inculcation in these people of the belief that their languages and cultures were benighted and pre-modern, and that political and social maturity required abandoning them in order to remake themselves in the image of their colonial rulers.

Nation-building of the kind that was carried out in the XIXth and early XXth centuries in European countries such as France had similar cultural agendas. For the sake of the creation and spread of a single *lingua franca* across the state's territory, and the creation of a single national identity, schools were prohibited by central authorities from teaching regional languages such as Breton and Corsican, which were also represented to their speakers as inferior to the metropolitan language and culture.

Let me refer to the kinds of cases in which speakers of weaker languages undergo significant pressures to go over to stronger languages with which they coexist in linguistic space for a variety of reasons – geographical, sociological, sociolinguistic – which do *not* include the intention on the part of some powerful linguistic agent to assimilate the weaker one as 'mere number cases' (Weinstock forthcoming). Let me refer to the kinds of cases in which these pressures are at least in part due to the kind of highly paternalistic imposition of colonial or metropolitan languages upon other language groups as 'colonial cases'.

It is clear that the kinds of background conditions of justice that as we saw are according to Rawls a condition for the social bases of self-respect do not obtain in colonial cases. Colonial situations (and, I would argue, aggressive nation-building cases) are defined by the imposition of the will of a stronger group upon a weaker group, and are premised on the ability of the former group to generate a sense of worthlessness and inferiority on the part of the weaker group.

That injustice is present in 'mere number cases' is at the very least open to question. In such cases, speakers respond not to coercion or to the deliberate attempt on the part of a more powerful group to demean and disparage, but rather to a more impersonal set of sociolinguistic forces. Indeed, where two groups of different sizes coexist and interact, the pressure for members of the smaller group to learn and speak the bigger language will make itself felt, even in the absence of a 'colonizing' intent on the part of the latter.

The question of whether the persistence of such 'mere number' inequalities in the absence of any measures to remediate for their effects represents injustice is too large a question to address in the context of this article. The point I want to make here is that it is quite difficult for Van Parijs to appeal to the injustice of unremediated mere number cases, since the very processes that are at work in such cases are the ones that Van Parijs points to as responsible for the (desirable) spread of English as a global *lingua franca*. Were the simple fact that English benefitted from its numerical supremacy sufficient to make the processes that lead to its spread incompatible with the social bases of self respect, it would follow that not just the erosion of a language, but also the spread of English as a *lingua franca* would have to be looked upon askance by Van Parijs. Clearly, 'mere number' cases must be viewed from within Van Parijs' theory as largely benign, lest he undercut the basis of his support for the spread of English as a *lingua franca*.

The language that Van Parijs uses to characterize the relationship between speakers of stronger and weaker languages brought into interaction by circumstances suggests that he realizes that the operation of sociolinguistic processes in the context of mere number cases does not in and of itself bespeak the kind of absence of respect that might erode a group's self-esteem. In a telling paragraph, he writes:

> If they [the speakers of a stronger language] do not bother to learn the local language, if instead they require the locals to use their own language when interacting with them [...] the suspicion can legitimately arise that there is some arrogance involved, some lack of respect, a denial of parity of esteem, *not fundamentally different from one associated with the relationship between a colonizer and the population being colonized.* (Van Parijs 2011, p. 141; emphasis added)

If Van Parijs is claiming here that acting on the basis of the kinds of incentives that are present in mere number cases is tantamount to the kind of contempt and sense of cultural superiority that characterizes colonialism, then surely he is guilty of overstatement. As he himself recognizes a few sentences later, sociolinguistic dynamics on the one hand, and attitudes of arrogance and cultural superiority on the other, are logically distinct, though he is undoubtedly correct in claiming that in cases in which linguistic pressure results in the main from the former rather than the latter, 'a set of real *or imaginary* historical *episodes* and *anecdotes* often feeds the *suspicion* that arrogance is an important factor, if not the main one' (Van Parijs 2011, p. 141; emphasis added). The point I want to make here is one which Van Parijs ultimately seems to agree with: whatever the *suspicion* that may arise as a result of the operation of sociolinguistic forces that those who benefit from them are guilty of arrogance or even worse, of 'colonial' attitudes, it is in principle possible to distinguish cases in which threats to language occur as a result of intentional human action grounded in contemptuous attitudes, from ones in which people simply respond to the incentive structure present in mere number cases. Reverting to the Rawlsian analysis briefly mooted above, the social bases of self-respect are compromised when people are coerced into abandoning their languages because they find themselves oppressed by colonial or metropolitan rulers. To claim that they are compromised when speakers of weak and large languages simply respond to the incentives that are presented by mere number cases is a much more ambitious claim, one that as we have seen is difficult to square with his celebration of the forces that have led English to its predominant place as the global *lingua franca*. People may sometimes *feel* in such cases as if the social bases of self-respect are lacking, but in the absence of some identifiable injustice, such feelings cannot be taken to be self-validating.

The argument from parity of self-esteem thus has a more limited range of application than advertised. It applies to colonial cases, but cannot be taken from within the context of Van Parijs' theory to apply to mere number cases. One way in which to respond to this is to say that in fact the two sets of cases are extensionally, though not intensionally equivalent. The claim would be that mere number cases result from colonial cases, such that the former preserve the moral 'taint' of the latter. On this view, languages such as English may very well benefit from being the 'winners' of impersonal sociolinguistic processes, but their having achieved a position that allows them to benefit in this manner is the result of the spread of language through colonial or metropolitan oppression. The domination of languages such as English would thus be incompatible with parity of respect because of the circumstances under which it achieved the position that then allowed it to benefit from the operation of predictable causal forces.

Determining the point at which the stain of historical injustice ceases is a vexed question, one which, again, I cannot hope to do justice to here (Ives 2010). Suffice it to say that Van Parijs in his support of English as a *lingua franca* insists upon separating out questions about the historical origins of the rise of English to dominance, and of the ideological freight that English may still carry in virtue of that dominance, from questions about the usefulness of English as a vehicle for progressive political causes. To the contingent connection between English and colonialism and/or global capitalism, Van Parijs argues that the appropriate response 'consists in appropriating the emerging lingua franca in order to disseminate with its help whatever content we see fit' (Van Parijs 2011, p. 33). If anything, Van Parijs is therefore inclined to the view that the use of a language that has been the cultural vehicle for oppression and domination can be turned around against those who would use it for unjust causes. Speakers of weaker languages can in his view be agents rather than merely passive subjects in the face of attempted linguistic domination. The use of languages associated with domination is thus not incompatible with the social bases of self-respect. *A fortiori*, the use of languages associated with injustice in the past is not something about which speakers of smaller languages need hang their heads in shame. The degree to which it is compatible with self-respect thus depends in Van Parijs' view on the question of whether progressive use can be made of such languages.

Thus, the range of cases in which the argument from parity of self-esteem applies is limited to those in which people legitimately come to feel that they are being treated as less than equal, not because of the operation of an incentive structure that might make it more difficult for them than for others to resist the lure of other languages, and to have others gravitate toward theirs, but rather because they are being treated unjustly. It is when unjust background conditions obtain that people have reason to feel as if they are being treated as less than full equals. Taking their feelings of lack of parity of self-esteem as being anything more than evidential is a case of the tail wagging the dog.

I have argued thus far that Van Parijs has not shown that 'mere number' cases evidence the kind of injustice that might trigger justifiable feelings of lack of parity of self-esteem. I would like to end this section by asking the following question, however: does it matter? Does the justification of the kinds of measures that he envisages in order to allow a group to protect its language against the sociolinguistic pressures it would otherwise be subject to depend upon its being able to show that it has principled ground to do so, based upon its being to parity-of-esteem-inhibiting injustice?

I don't think that it does. Rather than grounding the right of a linguistic group to enact legislation to protect its language upon prior injustice (a justification which, as I have suggested, would not apply to 'mere number' cases), a linguistic group that finds itself on the wrong side of a 'mere numbers' asymmetry can very well do so on the basis of the value of democracy and self-determination. In the same way that it can decide to invest more or less in its public transport system, or in its public libraries, or in its parks, on the basis of the results of democratic deliberation and democratic processes, a group can decide to enact legislation aimed at protecting its vulnerable language against the predictable impact of interaction with other, stronger languages. Between the area of policies that political entities are *prohibited* from adopting for reasons of basic political morality, and policies that they are *required* to enact for similar kinds of reasons, there lies the vast area of policies that groups *may* choose to enact. Now, different groups whose languages are made vulnerable by interaction with other groups may present quite different distributions of linguistic preferences among its members. In some such groups, a majority of members may feel quite indifferent about whether its language survives over time or not (whether or not its vulnerable position results from unjust background circumstances or from mere number). Indeed, some may welcome the advent of a language that allows them to communicate more widely. The attachment of many of its members to the patrimonial tongue may be sufficiently weak that it at the end of the day does not care much whether the sociolinguistic processes leading to bilingualization end up eroding their native language over time.

For others, however, the distribution of such preferences may make it the case that a majority of citizens consider the protection of their patrimonial tongue to be a political priority. It is in such circumstances perfectly legitimate for the group to enact legislation aimed at achieving that end. A set of policies with this aim would fall within the sphere of a group's democratic discretion. It could enact it without having to point to any past wrongdoing on the part of third parties.

Now, a group that wanted its language laws to fall within broadly liberal democratic norms would have to ensure that such policies satisfied criteria of proportionality. That is, to the extent that they involved coercing citizens, whether newcomers, indigenous linguistic minorities, or its own native speakers, into adopting linguistic behavior that it would not otherwise adopt, they would have to be relatively parsimonious. In particular, it would have to be able to show that its coercive legislation does not limit the language rights of citizens any more than is strictly required in order to achieve its legislative end. Moreover, it would have to accept the liberal principle that there is a point at which the restriction of freedoms is so severe as to no longer be justifiable by *any* such end. But on the assumption that its legislation did fall within these bounds, language laws aimed at protecting language from sociolinguistic forces tending toward unilingualism are justifiable on liberal-democratic grounds even in 'mere number' cases, that is, even in the absence of injustice. Thus, it could very well be that at the end of the day, the argument from parity of self-esteem is something of a red herring.

The limits on linguistic territoriality

The take-home claim of the foregoing section of this paper is that injustice rather than mere differences of size justifies linguistic groups in appealing to the LT principle in order to offset processes that might lead their group to being linguistically assimilated. The simple operation of sociolinguistic mechanisms is not obviously incompatible with the social bases of self-esteem. At any rate, it is difficult for Van Parijs to make the claim that they are, given the degree to which he views them as benign in creating the conditions for the emergence of a global *lingua franca*.

In this section, I want to turn to another question. Will the LT principle be effective in offsetting the tendency to linguistic erosion that can result from the operation of sociolinguistic mechanisms, from injustice, or from a complex intertwining of the two?

To a large degree, this is an empirical question. Much will hinge on empirical sets of circumstances that will differ from case to case: the relative economic power of the contending linguistic groups, the difference in size, etc. But there are reasons to think that Van Parijs exaggerates the effectiveness of the LT principle. Or to put the point with greater precision, there are reasons to think that he exaggerates the degree to which the LT principle will be able to give rise to the desired result – the stabilization of an otherwise vulnerable language – in the absence of illiberal policies being adopted within the territory that the threatened linguistic community has 'grabbed'. Let me explain.

The point of the LT principle is not simply to erect political borders around the territory occupied by a linguistic group. Rather it is to provide the group with powers to enact coercive linguistic legislation within that territory. A liberal default position in the area of language policy might be to adopt what Van Parijs calls an 'accommodating linguistic regime', one in which the state in its official communications with its citizens and in its organization of public services 'simply adjusts to the demand of the population' (Van Parijs 2011, p. 133). But a group whose members are vulnerable to the lure of a stronger language, and which attracts immigrants who are even more vulnerable given the absence of any identity link with the language of the group into which they are immigrating, and which may also include more long-settled linguistic minorities (call them 'indigenous linguistic minorities'), must if it wants to preserve its language counteract these powerful incentives by lashing its own members to the linguistic mast, and by forcing immigrants to assimilate into the smaller language that they would otherwise not feel the pull of. Depending on the size of the indigenous linguistic minorities, the effectiveness of coercive language measures may have to be extended to them as well, though the iteration of the 'grab a territory' principle makes the justification of the coercion of such minorities more difficult.

Van Parijs very helpfully distinguishes four dimensions along which language policy regimes will differ in their coerciveness – extension, ambition, generality, and severity. A language policy is more or less extensive depending on the number of contexts to which it applies. It is more or less ambitious depending on the number of languages that it requires that people learn and use. Its generality depends upon the degree to which it makes exceptions or not for certain categories of residents. And its severity depends upon the nature of the sanctions that are visited upon contravenors.

Let's assume, in the first instance, that a language policy need not be too coercive along any of these dimensions in order to ensure compliance of native speakers. They will on plausible cultural and psychological assumptions have independent reason to want to be able to use their mother tongue as a public language. Arguably, they face an assurance problem: they will make use of the language given sufficient assurance that others will as well. Given this antecedent preference, sanctions presumably need not be very severe in order to provide the needed counterweight to the attraction of the stronger language.

But things will be different for immigrants, or for indigenous linguistic minorities, who do not speak the language of the group attempting to stabilize its language as a mother tongue. They are unlikely to have identity-based reasons to speak the language of the group. Their linguistic repertoire will be guided to a greater degree than will be the case for the members of the language group in question by instrumental considerations. The stronger language from which the speakers of the weaker language are trying to immunize themselves will loom large in their calculations, or at least, it will loom larger than it will for speakers of the 'weaker' language.

In an accommodating linguistic regime, chances are that immigrants will learn just enough of the weaker language to get by minimally just in those institutional contexts in which they are required to receive services in that language. Given the limited resources, in terms of time and money, that they have in order to develop their linguistic repertoire, they will in the absence of countervailing incentives or coercion be likely to invest as little as is feasible in the weaker language. What's more, a mild coercive regime of the kind that might be sufficient to keep native speakers from succumbing to the attraction of the stronger language may very well be insufficient to modify the incentives of immigrants or other linguistic minorities substantially.

This may lead to a version of Laponce's law even for a language group that has acted on the LT principle, and enacted coercive legislation on the territory over which they have jurisdiction. Immigrants and members of indigenous linguistic minorities are likely to be far less proficient in the weaker than in the stronger language. What's more, they will, whatever their level of linguistic competence in the weaker language, only *use* that language in the contexts in which they are legally required to on pain of sanction. In virtue of the lesser competence achieved by immigrants and native linguistic minorities in the local language, and of their lesser willingness to make use of that language outside of legally mandated contexts, it is quite likely that speakers of the weaker language will find themselves speaking with immigrants in the stronger language if they want to be able to communicate with them effectively. (The severity with which Laponce's law will take hold obviously depends upon a number of contextual variables, such as the number of immigrants taken in, their relative economic power, and the like).

But this tendency may very well lead to the thought that the attainment of the objective of language stabilization will require an increase in the language regime's coercive character. If immigrants do not achieve more than a functional competence in the weaker language, and choose to use another language in contexts in which they are not forced to use the 'official' one, then the temptation may grow to increase the number of contexts in which they are forced to use it (thus increasing the coercive regime's 'extension'). The temptation may make itself felt to close loopholes that temporary residents may be inclined to exploit to remove themselves from the ambit of the law. Increased sanctions may also be employed in order to tarnish the luster that use of the stronger language may have.

The temptation may also be to create bulwarks against the operation of Laponce's law by modifying the majority linguistic community's susceptibility to it. If the speakers of the threatened language also have proficiency in the 'stronger' language toward which immigrants and indigenous linguistic minorities gravitate, this will provide fertile ground for the operation of erosive sociolinguistic forces such as Laponce's law. A part of the solution might therefore be to limit the access of members of the threatened linguistic community to the 'stronger' language (for example, by delaying the point at which it is taught in schools, by teaching it poorly or insufficiently, by dubbing movies and TV shows, etc.).

At a certain point, the increase in the coerciveness of the linguistic regime may become too costly from the point of view of liberal rights and freedoms. Language stabilization cannot be taken as an end that justifies all means. There exists a point on the spectrum of coercion where gains in a language's ability to offset the corrosive influence of injustice, and/or of sociolinguistic mechanisms will exact too great a cost in terms of rights, at least for those of us inclined to believe that the pursuit of such goals should always be tempered by liberal-democratic norms.

How may a language policy veer into illiberality? In a number of ways. For example, it can by extending the contexts within which citizens are obligated by law to use the weaker language erode the degree to which they are able to make private decisions about language. A liberal society allows its citizens to live according to their conceptions of the good and their values. The ability to make some non-trivial use of whatever language one chooses is surely part of what is required in order for a society to respect its citizens as authors of their own lives.

Another way in which a state can fall foul of liberal principles through coercive legislation has to do not so much with the way in which it treats immigrants and indigenous linguistic minorities, but rather in the way in which it treats mother-tongue speakers of the weaker language. It can, for example, prevent them from accessing stronger languages through the educational system. Given the opportunities that competence in the *lingua franca* affords, it would be limiting the horizons of citizens to too great a degree to deny them access. In particular, given the competence that other members of the society in question have in the larger question, such a policy may end up violating the principle of equality of opportunity.

Finally, as was mentioned above, the temptation might arise to limit the access of members of the threatened linguistic community to potentially corrosive stronger languages. This might occur by delaying the point at which children have access to it through the education system. I have argued elsewhere that such a restriction risks violating the principle of equality of opportunity, as children would find themselves deprived of an important tool that they might need in order to carry out their plans of life (Weinstock 2011).

I can't go into detail as to precisely where the line at which a coercive language policy shades into illiberality is situated. It is quite likely that no such bright lines exist, and that certain kinds of policies that are located close to the line will be the subject of reasonable disagreement. The points I wanted to make in this section was, first, that the LT principle, in and of itself, may be impotent to counter forces tending to corrode the language of a smaller language group, and that there is such point at which a non-accommodating regime will end up posing problems from the point of view of a liberal-democratic theory of justice. Such cases reveal that it is not the LT principle per se, but rather the coerciveness of the language laws that are enacted within the territory, that will determine the likelihood that a language will be able to offset these forces or not.

Conclusion

In this paper, I have attempted to do two things. First, I have argued that Van Parijs' justification for the LT principle on the basis of the notion of parity of self-esteem fails, because it fails to distinguish what I have here referred to as 'colonial' and 'mere number' cases. I have also argued that the importance of this conclusion may not be as great as might be supposed given the importance that Van Parijs ascribes to it in the overall argumentative economy of his book, because a group can decide to enact coercive legislation as a matter of democratic will, rather than for reasons of justice. A liberal democratic ethics will however require that it make use of coercion as parsimoniously as possible, and that it recognize that certain violations of individual rights cannot be undertaken, no matter what the consequences.

Second, I have argued that Van Parijs may underestimate the degree to which policies that respect these liberal democratic strictures will succeed in arresting the sociolinguistic processes that lead to the spread of English as a *lingua franca* just at the point at which it comes to threaten bilingualism. The main reason is that though moderate policies can increase the level of competence in the weaker language on a territory, they cannot increase the level of *use* of that language. Laponce's law may moreover still operate in a context in which, though immigrants and indigenous linguistic minorities are competent in the weaker language, they choose not to make use of it outside of contexts in which the law requires that they do so.

Ultimately, it could be that those who both want to protect a vulnerable language *and* cleave to broadly liberal democratic norms may have to accept a certain degree of *uncertainty* as to the viability of their language over time.

Then again, the history of human languages suggest that the acceptance of uncertainty and linguistic risk may be part of the human condition, rather than being reserved to a limited number of particularly vulnerable languages.

Disclosure statement

No potential conflict of interest was reported by the author.

Note

1. The use of the terminology of 'weak' and 'strong' languages is borrowed from Van Parijs. As in his case, it is not meant to denote any qualitative evaluation.

Notes on contributor

Daniel Weinstock is the James McGill Professor in the Faculty of Law, McGill University. His work has ranged widely over many central issues in contemporary political philosophy, including nationalism, federalism, and the liberal management of multiculturalism. More recently, he has published a number of essays on the political philosophy of childhood and the family, on cities as sites of normative thinking, and on the philosophical underpinnings of public health policy.

References

Ives, P., 2010. Cosmopolitanism and global English: language politics in globalisation debates. *Political studies*, 58 (3), 516–535.
Van Parijs, P., 2011. *Linguistic justice for Europe and for the world*. Oxford: Oxford University Press.
Rawls, J., 1971. *A theory of justice*. Cambridge, MA: Harvard University Press.
Weinstock, D., 2011. Do the interests of children pose a limit on cultural rights? *In*: E. Rude-Antoine and M. Pievic, eds. *Éthique et famille* [Ethics and family]. Paris: L'Harmattan, 53–70.
Weinstock, D., forthcoming. The case of mere numbers. *In*: Y. Peled and D. Weinstock, eds. *Language ethics*.

The political value of languages

Rainer Bauböck

European University Institute, Florence, Italy

A theory of linguistic justice needs to take into account the three distinct values of language as a medium for communication, as a source of individual identity and as an instrument for political self-government. Doing so would undermine Van Parijs' claim that political borders and peoples should be downgraded to a purely instrumental role for purposes of social justice. But it would widen the scope of egalitarian global justice by including a universal right of individuals to membership self-governing polities and it could provide more solid theoretical foundations for his defence of coercive territorial language regimes.

Why should it matter for social justice what language people speak? Philippe Van Parijs' book provides three convincing reasons why. First, a common language enables persons deprived of fair opportunities to make their claims understood by others and to join deliberations about political responses to unequal opportunities. Second, people whose native language is a widespread lingua franca enjoy undeserved advantages because they do not need to invest into learning another language and – more significantly – because they have privileged access to jobs and markets for which skills in the lingua franca are needed. Third, if the speakers of a dominant language expect all others to communicate with them in that language, this asymmetry undermines equality of respect and dignity in a way that can only be overcome through protecting weaker languages rather than assimilating their speakers into a dominant one.

These core arguments of Van Parijs' book may seem rather uncontroversial. What makes his argument really exciting is the author's ingenuity in fleshing out institutional arrangements and public policies that could support linguistic justice in all three senses. In a collection of essays published in the same year as 'Linguistic Justice', he calls his approach the 'Rawls-Machiavelli' programme (Van Parijs 2011). The Rawlsian element of this programme is the idea that justice is the 'first virtue of social institutions' and that a theory of justice ought to apply therefore primarily to the basic structure of a society.

Yet 'Linguistic Justice' spends only few pages in Chapter 3 on discussing alternative principles of distributive justice and gives hardly any space to Rawlsian ideal theory. The starting point of the book is instead an empirical fact: the rapid spread of English as a global lingua franca and its implications for social justice. The Machiavellian part of the project consists in asking how democracy can be made to serve justice. Democratic institutions and policies should be designed in such a way that they are likely to generate just outcomes, just as Machiavelli believed that political institutions should be designed to enhance the fortune and glory of the city republic. Applying this approach to linguistic justice leads to sometimes quite striking policy prescriptions and Van Parijs does not shy away from summarising these in catchy slogans: 'ban dubbing' of English movies in order to lower the costs for learning the global lingua franca in the non-Anglophone world (pp. 108–113); 'poach the internet' to deprive Anglophones of some of their undeserved global market advantage in the media industries (pp. 78–82); make 'every language a queen' in its territory in order to protect it against colonisation by stronger languages in the local or global neighbourhood.

Readers who are sceptical about normative theorising and academic policy prescriptions will still find enough in this book to admire, such as the lucid explanatory analysis of language spread through 'probability-driven language learning' (pp. 11–13) and a 'maxi-min rule for language use', according to which among multilingual persons the language chosen for communication will normally be the one that is best known by the member of the audience who knows it least well (pp. 13–15). Equally compelling is the conceptual analysis of linguistic diversity in Chapter 6 that explores systematically the toolbox provided by biologists while at the same time showing how languages are disanalogous with biological species because their boundaries blur through dialectical continuity and lexical borrowing (pp. 179–181).

Readers whose main interest is in the normative argument may find that there is one ambition in this ambitious book that does not fully meet its goal: the attempt to reconcile the first two arguments in which language figures as a medium of communication with the third one in which it is a marker of collective identity. This is partly due to the fact that Van Parijs' background conception of justice has evolved since he published 'Real Freedom for All' (Van Parijs 1995). He now complements his view on distributive social justice with a norm of 'parity of esteem' that acknowledges misrecognition as a source of injustice and that was absent in his earlier work. Yet the theoretical elaboration and integration of this aspect into his broader theory of justice remain still somewhat rudimentary.

In this review essay, I will argue that Van Parijs should travel a bit further on the Machiavellian road by regarding democracy not only as an instrument for social justice, but embracing also to some extent Machiavelli's republican ideas about the intrinsic value of self-government. This would lead him to acknowledge that languages have not only communicative value in the sense of providing access to social and economic opportunities and identity value in the sense of providing individuals with a source of self-esteem, but also collective political value by providing territorial communities with boundary markers and enabling them to develop public spheres for deliberation about their common good. In other words, languages are also tools for self-government. I am going to argue that from this perspective, the right to establish a particular language in a territory may be nothing but a legitimate outcome of democratic procedures that have been suitably constrained by linguistic freedoms and minority rights. The defence of territorially coercive language regimes, which Van Parijs argues on ground of parity of esteem for individuals, is in my view thus more convincing and straightforward when building a basic right to self-government into our conception of justice. I will briefly elaborate the implications of this view for global justice and the construction of a European polity before discussing how it supports official language regimes at state and substate levels.

Stanley's other question

Because liberals are generally committed to a *Grundnorm* of equal respect and dignity for human beings, every liberal theory of justice must include an account of global justice. Liberals disagree about the extent to which requirements of domestic justice within liberal polities differ from those of global justice. One way of teasing out these disagreements is by looking at the role that liberal theorists attribute to particular political communities. John Rawls proposed a two-stage approach, with a liberal theory of social justice applying to the citizens of closed societies at the first stage and a theory of international justice applying to peoples at the second stage (Rawls 1999). Van Parijs takes the opposite side in this debate by starting from a theory of justice that is global in scope and moving from there to more contextualised accounts of domestic justice.

Although all reasonable theories acknowledge in some way that citizens of democratic states have some special rights and obligations that differ from what human beings owe to all other human beings, the starting point matters. Van Parijs' starting point is very explicitly global egalitarian justice: 'Any honest attempt to think seriously about justice for our century must downgrade nations and states from the ethical framework to the institutional toolkit' (p. 26). What it means to put nations and states into the institutional toolkit is spelled out more fully towards the end of the book: 'Nations, politically organised peoples ... are sheer instruments to be created and dismantled, structured and absorbed, empowered and constrained, in the service of justice in a sense that far from reduces to fundamental liberties' (p. 139). From a perspective of global egalitarian justice, Van Parijs invites us to redesign nation states and their borders so that social justice can be achieved as 'real freedom for all' and not just for the lucky citizens of wealthy democracies.

He illustrates the importance of a global lingua franca for this perspective through the story of 'Stanley', a Nigerian boy who asks Van Parijs shortly before he catches a plane to Europe why he (the boy) cannot come with him (Van Parijs) to wealthy Belgium. That he could not give an honest answer keeps haunting Van Parijs, but that the boy could ask him this question serves to show how social justice is no longer a purely domestic matter and why a shared global lingua franca is important for creating a 'global justificatory community' (pp. 24–27).

Does it follow that nations, states and their borders must be downgraded to the institutional toolkit for delivering global justice? I do not think so. We can imagine Stanley asking a slightly different question: 'How come your country is so much richer than mine?' Or in other words: 'Why don't I have the same opportunities in my country that other boys have in yours?' This question, too, presupposes a global justificatory community that can be more easily brought about if there is a common lingua franca. The two questions should not even be regarded as alternative ones. Stanley may have justice-based claims that other states should keep their borders open *and* that he should not be condemned to poverty in the country where he has grown up. In fact, if the second question could be successfully addressed, the first one would be much easier to answer too. In a world where people are no longer pushed to seek their chances across borders because they need to escape from violence or poverty, wealthy and rich countries could no longer argue that they need to restrict immigration for the sake of maintaining decent standards of social justice for their citizens and residents. In spite of all its conflicts and setbacks, this is the basic lesson of European integration. Where states meet certain economic and democratic standards and agree to a certain level of supranational economic and political integration, free movement across open borders can become an institutional right of supranational citizenship rather than just a moral claim.

Stanley's two questions are thus not mutually exclusive, but the second one implies a quite different perspective on global justice in which politically organised people are not regarded as mere tools for global justice, but as the primary addressees of their residents' claims. This view is not at all opposed to duties of global justice, but directs these towards the goal of enabling[1] other societies to govern themselves in ways that promotes the autonomy and well-being of their members. Stanley's other question has been asked in different contexts. Colonialism gave rise to claims of self-determination directly addressed to a particular colonial power. Globalisation changes the context for self-government by creating a multitude of secondary addressees: the community of states and its international organisations, the most powerful states, such as the US and China, regional associations of states, such as the EU, as well as global corporations. In other words, an account of global justice that takes seriously Stanley's hypothetical second question will have to attribute much stronger value to membership in political communities than Van Parijs seems ready to accept.

Van Parijs could respond that he does not at all ignore the value of self-government, since he regards the emergence of a global justificatory community that is facilitated through the spread of English as a mere precondition for the building of transnational demoi and eventually a global demos that have capacities for political deliberation and mobilisation across borders (pp. 27–28). So why can't Stanley ask his two questions as a citizen of the world rather than of Nigeria? The difficulty with this suggestion is that transnational democracy can only work if it builds on more comprehensive self-government within the boundaries that are being transcended. A conception of global justice that defends a universal right to membership in a self-governing polity must affirm first the need for boundaries that demarcate the territorial jurisdiction and membership in such polities before it can argue that they should be as open as possible for transborder migration and deliberation.[2]

This view does not entail a defence of the present borders and powers of states. These may well be challenged as illegitimate or unjust. Yet such challenges will in most cases be articulated as particular claims to self-government rather than as demands for global social justice. Clearly, not all contestations of present borders can be presumed to be legitimate. But the test for their legitimacy cannot be which border is more conducive to delivering social justice. We need to ask instead which territorial arrangement accommodates competing claims to self-government in such a way that it deserves to be supported by all. If borders were just a tool for achieving social justice, should we then always aim for the widest possible, that is global, scope of inclusion or construct instead rather small political communities that can generate stronger solidarity among their members and thereby enhance compliance with redistributive duties? Given the indeterminacy of solutions to this trade-off and the high transaction costs of border changes, isn't the view that borders are mere instruments for social justice likely to end up – paradoxically – defending the present borders of states?

The tower of Brussels and the territorial fortresses of national languages

The beautiful cover of Van Parijs' book shows a photo-collage of Brussels houses with the EU Council and Commission buildings on top in an arrangement that alludes to Pieter Brueghel's painting of the Tower of Babel. It is a very appropriate metaphor for the official language regime of the EU analysed in Chapter 4 of the book. In this chapter, Van Parijs largely refrains from normative critique and confines himself to a penetrating analysis of the dilemma between the need for equal recognition of all official languages of the member states, on the one hand, and the need for reducing translation and interpreter costs and promoting ease of communication and deliberation through the wider use of English, on the other hand. With every accession that adds a new language to the official repertoire, the costs of official plurilingualism increase exponentially, so the drift towards wider use of the de facto lingua franca is inexorable.

Van Parijs' proposed solution is that member states should be willing to pay for the costs of interpreter services and translations. While this seems reasonable for internal deliberations – including those in the plenary of the European Parliament – where effective communication is more important than symbolic representation, I disagree that official translations of EU legislation into all EU languages will become redundant with wider knowledge of English and are anyhow problematic because they undermine consistency in the interpretation of legal norms (pp. 124–125). It seems incoherent to defend the right of states to establish official languages in their territories but to accept that EU decisions that directly apply to these states and their citizens remain exempt from that territorial language regime. The false perception that EU decisions are taken 'in Brussels' entirely separate from domestic political agendas can only be reinforced if the former are communicated exclusively in English while the latter are stated and debated in national languages.

The EU language regime provides the first illustration of the parity of esteem principle that Van Parijs subsequently applies to the coercive language regimes of states. I find his argument generally convincing in the former, but unconvincing in the latter context. Equality in the sense of parity of esteem between the member states and – as the EU Treaty says[3] – their national identities – is a basic principle of the EU's constitution. Because the EU is a Union of member states, this parity of esteem is not extended to all individual citizens as speakers of different languages. Only those languages recognised as official ones by the member states also become official languages of the EU. Catalan, although it is spoken by many more EU citizens than Maltese, can only get limited recognition 'on condition that the Spanish government foots the bill (p. 127)'. In a compound polity like the EU, parity of esteem for languages applies nearly exclusively at the federal level, that is between constituent polities rather than between individual citizens.

Van Parijs devotes Chapter 5, the longest in his book, to a defence of protectionist regimes for national languages within states on grounds of parity of esteem. He starts by distinguishing accommodation regimes from coercive ones. The former would merely provide fair background conditions for a free competition between languages, while the latter use state coercion to support specific languages by prescribing their use in public contexts either for certain categories of speakers – a non-territorial form of coercion – or within a territory. The empirical evidence is clear: all modern states have established coercive territorial regimes, with accommodating or categorical ones playing at best a supplementary role. It is also clear that the EU regime is neither accommodating nor coercive in this way. It is simply a system of mutual recognition between languages that have been territorially established in the member states.

When applied to individuals, parity of esteem is an intuitively attractive principle because it recognises that languages do not only have instrumental value for individuals as tools of communication, but also identity value. Even a second or third language that one has learnt at a later stage in life may carry some of this value for persons who take pride in mastering it, especially as authors, but more generally, it is the first language that has the greatest identity value for most people.

Parity of esteem is a perfectly plausible principle for accommodating language regimes in which states stay as neutral as possible, given the general constraints that languages cannot be fully disestablished since governments have to communicate with residents and that costs of multilingual public services increase with the number of languages. In such a regime, immigration of a sufficiently large foreign language group would automatically be accommodated by including its language in the public provision of services in relation to their numbers. This represents an even-handed approach of '"pro-rated multilingualism", which may lead to the maintenance, expansion, or extinction of the various languages in competition' (p. 134).

We can find instances of linguistic accommodation in a rather diluted version in most democracies with large scale immigration. Public schools hire bilingual teachers who help the children of immigrants adapt to a dominant language; hospitals employ interpreters and bilingual nurses; public administrations translate forms and information sheets for their clients into immigrant languages; some US states even use bilingual ballots (in English and Spanish) in political elections, although these have been recently rolled back by a wave of 'official English' state legislation. What distinguishes these accommodative policies from Van Parijs' ideal-typical accommodating language regime is not merely their relatively marginal scope, it is also the justifying reason. In nearly all cases – and contrary to what the detractors of multiculturalism want to make us believe – the reason for accommodation is instrumental rather than a recognition of the deep identity value of immigrant languages. The main purpose of multilingual policies for immigrants is to facilitate communication and often it is also to facilitate the language shift. In other words, in immigration contexts, accommodation is never an even-handed policy that pays equal respect to all first languages based on their significance for individual identity, but always a secondary accommodation of linguistic diversity within a primary regime of territorial linguistic coercion.

Van Parijs offers three justifications for such language regimes. The first is to avoid 'colonial attitude' (p. 141). He illustrates it with the case of an American immigrant in Belgium who expects that natives learn enough English to communicate with him. In confrontation between stronger and weaker language, a territorially coercive regime for the weaker one 'avoids it being always the same group who does the linguistic bowing' (ibid.). The second reason is to avoid 'kindness-driven agony' (pp. 142–146). The more speakers of different languages interact and intermarry, the faster will the weaker languages be replaced by the stronger ones. Many liberals might think that such linguistic conversion is unobjectionable if it happens without coercion. However, Van Parijs' argues that 'each linguistic community should be allowed, consistently with fundamental rights, to design its institutions so as to preserve a linguistic and cultural heritage in which it takes a legitimate interest' (p. 142). Finally, the third argument is that local languages may not only be legitimately preserved if their current speakers are willing to bear the costs for these efforts, but that they can also be legitimately established as the *dominant* language in the territory: 'It constitutes an essential condition for the local language to be able to function fairly in the top function, that is as the medium for the local population *qua* political community' (pp. 146–147). In a territorially differentiated coercive language regime 'every tongue [can be] a queen' somewhere and this secures parity of esteem between territorially established languages of the same kind that we find in the EU.

But how would the colonial attitude argument apply to immigrants who speak a weaker language, say Polish immigrants in the UK? On which ground can they be asked to pass an English test before acquiring British citizenship, as they now must? At this point, Van Parijs resorts to counterfactual reciprocity. '[C]oercive rules are justified on grounds of parity of esteem in so far as they are viewed as part of a global regime that incorporates an expectation of reciprocity. Parity of esteem can be served by the coercive protection of a particular language in a particular territory only if the native speakers of that language can be expected to comply symmetrically with the coercive protection of other languages in their own respective territories' (p. 149).

This is a sophisticated argument, but I do not think it succeeds. Territorial establishment of languages cannot be justified on grounds of parity of esteem because, as pointed out by Ernest Gellner (1983), there are many more languages than territories in which they could be established. Not even if we allow, as Van Parijs does, that territories are very unequal in size can the condition be met that 'all the languages involved must enjoy a similar protection' (p. 150).[4] We do not have to invoke the example of the Roma who do not have a homeland where their many different languages could be protected. Van Parijs' own analysis of linguistic diversity in Chapter 6 suggests that any attempt to divide territories in such a way that each language can be queen in at least one of them is bound to fail, unless we already preselect the languages that qualify for territorial establishment by a criterion of de facto dominance within a demarcated geographic region. Doing so would, however, make the argument largely circular, since the fact of dominance of particular languages in particular territories is generally the outcome of political processes of linguistic establishment.

The argument for territorial coercion on ground of parity of esteem is also implausible because the individual identity value of a first language does not depend much on whether and where it is territorially established. The daughter of Kurdish immigrants in Sweden may feel just as strongly that the language her parents spoke to her when she was little is an important part of her identity as does the son of Catalan parents growing up in Barcelona. Parity of esteem requires that coercive language regimes accommodate linguistic minorities and prevent their discrimination; it cannot justify why some languages but not others have a claim to establish a coercive regime. My objection is thus that parity of esteem between individuals as native speakers of strong and weak, territorially established and non-established, native and immigrant languages is strictly impossible to realise. Territorial disestablishment for the sake of introducing a general accommodation regime would approximate parity of esteem in the sense of political neutrality, but such parity would come at the price of very little social esteem for any language that does not serve as a lingua franca.

As an alternative justification for coercive territorial regimes, I propose to recognise the collective political value of languages as tools for building self-governing polities. This value is entirely instrumental. Languages are used politically for governing populations but also to strengthen their sense of collective identity. It might thus seem that the political value of languages is analogous to their instrumental and identity value for individuals. Yet, unless we adopt a Herderian view of peoples, political collectives are social constructs without a natural self whose identity can be shaped by a native language. The political value of languages carries normative weight only if political self-government itself is regarded as valuable.

The political use of languages has an external and internal side. The external value lies in demarcating a territory and population that has a legitimate claim to self-government. Quebecois nationalists are much less interested in preserving the French language wherever it is spoken in Canada than in the territorial autonomy of Quebec province. French served well enough to lend plausibility to their claim that Quebec is a distinct society and they were quite willing to abandon Francophone populations outside the province. Much the same is true for Catalans in Spain. Today, the borders between independent states may be less contested than those inside plurinational and plurilingual states, but language difference has in many cases also been instrumentalized for drawing and justifying international borders. In a politically integrated EU with open internal borders, it is still crucial for sustaining a strong sense of distinct nationhood among the various peoples of Europe.

The internal political value of territorialized languages is quite obvious for governments who need to communicate with residents in order to enforce the law and provide public goods and services, but is even stronger for democratic citizens who want to participate in deliberations about the common good and hold governments accountable. Colonial and authoritarian governments have ruled multilingual societies through combined uses of a lingua franca within public administrations and accommodation of native languages in communication with subjects. It is the transformation of subjects into citizens with claims to representation that provides the strongest push towards coercive territorial language regimes. Although territorial self-government does not require institutional monolingualism, it needs either differentiated linguistic establishment in various parts of the territory or one or at most two shared languages spoken by most citizens throughout the territory.

Van Parijs may be ready to acknowledge the political value of languages for nation-building and democracy but ask why this should matter for a theory of justice. My answer is that justice does not require that all languages are similarly protected in their territories, but that individuals are similarly protected and equally respected as members of self-governing political communities. In a world that is politically structured into territorially bounded polities, the allocation of territorially differentiated self-government powers is a fundamental matter of justice just as much as equality of opportunity and respect for individual identities.

When discussing the legitimacy of Quebecois or Catalan language protection laws, we should not ask whether French and Catalan native speakers have stronger claims that their linguistic identities be publicly recognised than immigrants in these provinces. Instead, we need to consider whether the citizens of these provinces have a stronger claim to territorial self-government than the other Canadian provinces and Spanish autonomous communities. Their coercive language laws can only be justified if the answer is yes. The same logic applies to the establishment of national languages by states. Deviations from an accommodation regime that treats all languages in an even-handed manner are justified if preserving the territorial domination of a national language strengthens the capacity of citizens to govern themselves as members of a distinct political community.

This argument still needs to overcome an objection. The external and internal political values of territorially established languages are among the most important resources for self-government, but they are not strictly necessary conditions. Scotland does not need to establish Highland Gaelic in order to distinguish itself from England. If the Maltese government decided to disestablish the Maltese language and operate in English only, the island would not cease to govern to itself.

So how can we know whether linguistic coercion is actually needed for self-government? The answer is that as external observers, we cannot know. Only the citizens themselves can know and they do so through democratic procedures, the outcomes of which are legitimate language laws. At this point, a theory of substantive linguistic justice meets a theory of procedural democratic legitimacy. If the substantive justification of coercive territorial language regimes lies in their instrumental role for securing territorial self-government, then we can test the legitimacy of language laws by asking whether they are the result of a legitimate exercise of self-government powers. In other words, if the government institutions of a territorial polity are democratically legitimate, then they have the power to pass coercive language laws.

From a liberal perspective, democratic legitimacy is always constrained by rights. In the case of language laws, these constraints include linguistic toleration through civil liberties of free speech and association for all languages, accommodation of the communication needs of native speakers of foreign languages, protection of linguistic minority rights in the territory (which may again be based on territorial self-government) and respect of agreements with other levels of government (e.g. concerning the teaching of a second official language in public education). Only within such constraints should self-governing polities have the power to determine their own coercive language regimes. This power implies also that they are free to abandon or weaken the protection of a dominant language.

In such a legitimate coercive language regime, immigrants have no claim to territorially establish their own political communities and languages within a polity that admits them as individual newcomers. Such a claim would illustrate a 'colonial attitude' – not necessarily towards the language spoken by native citizens, but towards their right to self-government. Settled immigrants have instead a right to be admitted to citizenship. As new citizens they may campaign for a stronger recognition of their native languages. They are then in the same position as native citizens who might propose that a territorially coercive regime be weakened in favour of a more accommodative one that accelerates the use of English because they want to promote their children's career in a global market. The mix between an accommodative and a coercive regime should therefore be regarded as a democratic choice that is constrained by, but not derived from individual language rights.

Conclusions

In line with his Rawls-Machiavelli programme, Van Parijs' book shifts the debate in political theory from a focus on linguistic rights to a focus on linguistic justice (p. 90). The first four chapters of his book present a powerful argument why the spread of English as a global lingua franca is conducive for global and domestic social justice and democratisation of the European Union and how the transitory injustices that accompany the global English steamroller can be redressed. Van Parijs' argument for coercive territorial language regimes on grounds of parity of esteem reverts, however, to the idea of language rights. Parity of esteem for individuals who have been raised in different languages is indeed a strong argument for protecting and accommodating linguistic minorities. It cannot, however, justify the much stronger protection of dominant languages in territorially autonomous provinces or nation states.

I have therefore suggested that a theory of linguistic justice needs to take into account the three distinct values of language as a medium for communication, as a source of individual identity and as an instrument for political self-government. Doing so would undermine Van Parijs' claim that political borders and peoples should be downgraded to a purely instrumental role for purposes of social justice. But it would widen the scope of egalitarian global justice by including a universal right of individuals to membership self-governing polities and it could provide more solid theoretical foundations for his defence of coercive territorial language regimes.

Disclosure statement

No potential conflict of interest was reported by the author.

Notes

1. A more cautious version of the argument could follow a Poggean line in defending a negative duty of global justice not to obstruct the capacity of other societies to govern themselves (see Pogge 2002).
2. As helpfully pointed out by an anonymous reviewer, Van Parijs acknowledges that the ultimate aim of global distributive justice can only be approached gradually through promoting and protecting redistributive regimes at subnational, national and supranational levels (see e.g. Van Parijs 1992, Van Parijs and Vanderborght 2012). He accepts thus bounded solidarity among citizens as a feature of the present non-ideal world. My disagreement is that I regard a plurality of self-governing polities with specific citizenships as a background condition for justice and a structural feature of any desirable ideal world.
3. Consolidated Version of the Treaty on European Union and the Treaty on the Functioning of the European Union (Lisbon Treaty) Art. 4(2).
4. This difficulty is acknowledged by Alan Patten (2009, pp. 124–126) who defends a principle of equal recognition of languages that is similar to Van Parijs' parity of esteem.

Notes on contributor

Rainer Bauböck holds a chair in social and political theory at the Department of Political and Social Sciences of the European University Institute. His research interests are in normative political theory and comparative research on democratic citizenship, European integration, migration, nationalism and minority rights. Together with Jo Shaw (University of Edinburgh) and Maarten Vink (University of Maastricht), he coordinates the European Union Democracy Observatory on Citizenship at http://eudo-citizenship.eu.

References

Gellner, E., 1983. *Nations and nationalism*. Oxford: Blackwell.
Patten, A., 2009. Survey article: the justification of minority language rights. *Journal of Political Philosophy*, 17 (1), 102–128.
Pogge, T., 2002. *World poverty and human rights*. London: Polity.
Rawls, J., 1999. *The law of peoples*. Cambridge, MA: Harvard University Press.
Van Parijs, P., 1992. Commentary: citizenship exploitation, unequal exchange and the breakdown of popular sovereignty. *In*: Brian Barry and Robert E. Goodin, eds. *Free movement. Ethical issues in the transnational migration of people and of money*. University Park, PA: The Pennsylvania State University Press, 155–166.
Van Parijs, P., 1995. *Real freedom for all; what (if anything) can justify capitalism?* Oxford: Oxford University Press.
Van Parijs, P., 2011. *Just democracy: the Rawls-Machiavelli programme*. Colchester: ECPR Press.
Van Parijs, P. and Vanderborght, Y., 2012. Basic income in a globalized economy. *In*: B. Reynolds and S. Healy, eds. *Does the European social model have a future?* Dublin: Social Justice Ireland, 31–60.

Lingua franca and linguistic territoriality. Why they both matter to justice and why justice matters for both

Philippe Van Parijs

Hoover Chair of Economic and Social Ethics, University of Louvain, Louvain-la-Neuve, Belgium

The bottom line of my book *Linguistic Justice for Europe and for the World* (Oxford University Press, 2011, paperback 2015) can roughly be captured in the combination of two recommendations: that the democratization of competence English as a lingua franca should be fostered in Europe and elsewhere and that language communities should be allowed to protect their language against the invasion of English and other powerful languages by imposing their own language in public communication and public education within some territorial boundaries. Most of my critics attack one or the other of these recommendations and some question some of the presuppositions of my whole approach. In this response, I try to refute some of these critiques by clarifying my claims or spelling out my arguments, and I make whatever concessions I believe are required.

In *Linguistic Justice for Europe and for the World* (Van Parijs 2011a, henceforth *LJ*), I argue that the dissemination of English as a lingua franca needs to fostered, but also that the resulting dominance of English tends to create injustice in three senses: free riding or cooperative injustice, unequal opportunities or distributive injustice and the violation of parity of esteem. The strategies I recommend in order to address cooperative and distributive justice have one by-product in common: a further strengthening of the dominance of English. Linguistic justice, however, is also a matter of parity of esteem. And the strategy best suited to pursue justice in this sense, I argue, requires that one should allow all language communities to 'grab a territory', that is to impose their language in public education and public communication within some territorial boundaries. Hence, *LJ*'s bottom line could roughly be captured in the simple formula: lingua franca + linguistic territoriality.

Unsurprisingly, some of the contributors to the present volume object to the first element in this formula, while others object to the second. More surprisingly, some of them agree with one or both of these elements but challenge the justification I give for them. In this response, I shall address some of these critiques. By so doing, I shall do far less than full justice to the many insightful remarks to be found in this volume. I shall focus on the points on which I feel I need to make some significant concession or clarify some important misunderstanding, while hoping that, by so doing, I shall not dodge any fatal objection to any of my central claims.

Is English a fiction?

The most radical critique of my approach comes from Sue Wright and, more diffusely, Stephen May, who accuse me of unthinkingly taking over a conception of language that is linked to the ideology of nation building and out of touch with contemporary reality. Wright contrasts a conception of language as a *system* – a set of rules shared by a homogeneous linguistic community – and language as a *practice* – an activity of 'languaging' whereby people use a hybrid and variable repertoire in order to somehow manage to communicate with each other. The first conception, she says, is intrinsic in Saussure's concept of 'langue' or Chomsky's concept of 'competence', as imperfectly manifested in people's 'paroles' and 'performances'. It fits the ideal of nation builders who want to convince people that they belong to the same nation by making them believe that there is something like a single language called 'French' or 'German' or 'Danish', etc. sharply distinct from others and that they must all learn to speak it 'correctly'. By contrast, the second conception emphasizes the great variability and heterogeneity of human communicative practices. Such 'languaging' characterizes communication even in allegedly unilingual communities, but it is particularly salient in the era of globalization, with a high rate of transient migration and huge diasporas that remain connected to their roots.

Does my approach presuppose the first conception and, if it does, is it thereby made irrelevant to contemporary linguistic realities, as widely documented in the sociolinguistic literature? True, when referring to languages and linguistic communities, I use 'English', 'French', etc. as if each of these corresponded to a single system of rules fully shared by the corresponding set of people. But I neither wish nor need to deny the complexities emphasized by Wright and May. The contrast they rightly emphasize seems to me misleadingly formulated in terms of 'system' versus 'practice': there is no linguistic system without a linguistic practice that manifests it, and no linguistic practice that does not rely on one or more underlying phonological, syntactic and semantic systems. But I have no problem accepting that 'languaging' is more ubiquitous than ever. One of many implications is that when speaking of English as the emerging lingua franca, I should make clearer than I did in *LJ* that I am not speaking about a single object, itself identical with another single object attributed to all so-called native English speakers as their common mother tongue. It is rather a large, diverse and fuzzy set of systems of rules, themselves often quite fuzzy, that govern sequences of sounds and (more tightly) strings of letters, and one that is distinct from another set of systems of rules, hardly less large, diverse and fuzzy, that is commonly referred to as the native language of, say, the bulk of the population of the United Kingdom.

Thus, whenever *LJ* uses words like 'English', 'French', 'Mandarin', it is true that it suggests an homogeneity more congenial to nation builders than meaningful to sociolinguists. But the crucial question here is whether acknowledging this complexity, as sociolinguists rightly expect us to do, invalidates anything in the characterization of the injustices I identify or in the strategies I propose to address them, in particular, as regards the dominance of English. For example, Sue Wright aptly points out that languaging in English as a lingua franca also needs to be learned by native speakers of English: among members of the European Parliament, she argues, some Brits are definitely less effective users of English as a lingua franca than many of their continental colleagues.[1] As to Stephen May, he emphasizes that many varieties of native English are badly stigmatized and complains about my 'unwillingness to address the social, class, and contextual locatedness of high prestige English language varieties'.

I do not need to deny any of this. All I need to assume is that proximity between one's native repertoire and the competence required for effective lingua franca languaging remains a significant advantage *ceteris paribus*, whether as regards cooperative and distributive justice or as regards parity of esteem. In order to assess this assumption, one needs to answer questions such as the following. Is access to the lingua franca really not harder for the average French or Chinese peasant/academic than for the average British or American peasant/academic? And is it really equally easy or difficult for all native and non-native speakers of 'English' to view the latter as their language and make it part of their identity? Awareness of sociolinguistic complexities highlighted by Wright and May forces one to pay attention to intra-linguistic justice as well as too inter-linguistic justice (see De Schutter 2014) and to think about linguistic injustice generally in continuous rather than in discrete terms. But my aim was only to formulate as clearly and simply as possible the core of the issues of linguistic justice in each of my three interpretations. For such a purpose, abstracting from these complexities is justified as long as the factual assumption spelled out above can be sustained. Sociolinguistic description must instruct political philosophy, and philosophical thinking can inspire sociolinguistic research. But their jobs are different, and so is, therefore, what they are justified in leaving aside.

Can free riding by anglophones be just?

The rebuttal presented in the previous paragraph holds, I believe, with regard to each of the dimensions of the conception of justice I defend. But it may not hold with regard to all conceptions of linguistic justice. In particular from the standpoint of cooperative justice as interpreted by David Robichaud in his essay, sociolinguistic complexities may well make a crucial difference. Why? Robichaud takes issue with my view that the anglophones' free riding on the voluntary learning of English by non-anglophones constitutes *ipso facto* a cooperative injustice. To clarify the issue, it may be useful to distinguish interactive surplus and cooperative surplus. The interactive surplus generated by the (spontaneous or concerted) adoption of a the lingua franca is the aggregate benefit that would not exist in the absence of some people learning it as a second language and using it to interact with one another and with anglophones. The cooperative surplus generated by the (concerted) adoption of the lingua franca is the aggregate benefit that would not exist in the absence of a cooperative deal between anglophones and non-anglophones. If non-anglophones learn English en masse out of self interest – as I recognize is happening –, there is a huge interactive surplus part of which is enjoyed free of charge by anglophones, while the cooperative surplus may be zero or negligible in comparison.

In such a case, my view is that fairness requires a significant contribution by anglophones, whereas Robichaud's view is that it does not. Extending the demands of cooperative justice to the whole of the interactive surplus, he writes, is unacceptable 'if we want to maintain the individuals' freedom'. In defense of my view, I could only repeat what I write at the start of chapter 2 of *LJ*, including the analogy with the cleaning by my father-in-law, which Robichaud takes up. In a case such as the adoption of a lingua franca, where there is 'massive and protracted interaction with substantial contributions that are systematically one-sided and produce benefits that are eagerly (though often unwittingly) enjoyed', fairness requires a contribution by those who would otherwise enjoy a handsome free ride (*LJ*, p. 53). Adopting rules that would prevent them from getting away with this free ride would admittedly involve a restriction of freedom, as does any rule stipulating a fair sharing of benefits.

Interestingly, however, Robichaud argues that even on his far more restrictive view of the demands of cooperative justice, a contribution by anglophones to the learning effort of non-anglophones may be justified. This is the case if one gives up my 'optimistic' assumption about the ineluctability of sufficient convergence towards English as a lingua franca. First possibility: even though many millions of non-anglophones learn English spontaneously to some extent, it may be optimal for anglophones that even more learn it and to a greater extent, which they would not do in the absence of a cooperative deal involving some contribution by anglophones. As Robichaud points out, however, once hundreds of millions of non-anglophones have learned English, the marginal utility of one more learning it may quite quickly shrink into insignificance.

Second possibility, more intriguing, suggested by Robichaud: the benefit to the anglophones of non-anglophones learning English may go beyond their individual immediate interest in having more speech partners. It could encompass what I present as the chief reason for needing a lingua franca, namely as a precondition for an EU-wide or worldwide demos in which the weakest are empowered thanks to a cheap transnational medium of communication. Given that this demos in turn is meant to increase the political feasibility of greater distributive justice, this will not be an obvious selling point with comparatively wealthy anglophones communities. But perhaps this progress towards global justice can be viewed as part of a more abstract, less material notion of benefit, in which case there could again be a cooperative surplus exceeding substantially the interactive surplus: a surplus that would only arise as a result of anglophones agreeing to compensating non-anglophones for learning more English than they would in the absence of such compensation. Ingenious indeed, but too far-fetched to be very plausible, it seems to me.

However, Robichaud mentions a third possibility, more plausible than the other two, that relies on the sort of sociolinguistic complexity highlighted by Wright and May. The variety or varieties of English on which non-anglophones tend converge as one or more (regionally differentiated) lingua francas may not be optimal from the anglophones' standpoint, too distant from their own native variety and hence in need of being learned by them too. The interactive surplus spontaneously enjoyed by anglophones would not be small. But the cooperative surplus achievable through a deal involving some contribution on their part – possibly just in the form of free provision of audio-visual and written production (see *LJ*, §2.12) – is even larger. This provides a neat illustration, I believe, of how sociolinguistics and political philosophy can interact fruitfully. Taking the heterogeneity of 'English' into account has no major impact on the implications of my conception of cooperative justice in the linguistic domain. But it is crucial to create a significant gap between the interactive surplus and the cooperative surplus, and thereby to trigger the anglophones' obligations of cooperative justice in Robichaud's conception.

Is a lingua franca really needed?

The other contributors to this volume are not worried about speaking about languages in the same simplified way as *LJ* does. This tends to make conversation easier but not necessarily agreement. Let us start with the spreading of the lingua franca. I do claim that it is not only happening, but that it should be accelerated. Denise Réaume strongly disagrees for at least four reasons.

Firstly, I do not pay proper attention to the fact that the dominance of English stems less from the maxi-min dynamics of communication than 'from the economic, political and cultural power of, first, the British Empire, and more lately the American empire'.[2] I do indeed claim than the quick spreading of competence in English among the younger generation of Europeans is driven by what I call the maxi-min dynamics, that is the self-reinforcing process that combines on the one hand, a strong tendency to use the language best known by the conversation partner who knows it least well and on the other, a strong tendency to learn those languages one has the highest probability of

LINGUISTIC JUSTICE

using. But I am not claiming that this dynamics operates in a power vacuum. Réaume concedes that I 'acknowledge that power plays some role in this history'. Indeed I devote a whole section to it (LJ, §1.8). But if a situation, such as the dominance of English, 'might not exist if not for unjust power relations that brought it into being', I should not restrict the scope of linguistic justice, she says, to the determination of 'how best to compensate for the way things turned out'. I should also address the economic and political inequalities of power that are at the root of today's unjust state of affairs. What might this mean?

I doubt Réaume believes that we should endeavor to realize the linguistic state of affairs which would have prevailed had no Germanic tribe invaded the British Isles in the fifth century or no French troops conquered Quebec in the seventeenth. More plausibly, she must mean that a crucial task, if only because of its impact on linguistic justice, is to fight for greater social justice, both within and across nations. If this is her view, I could not agree more. But this is precisely what lies at the heart of my plea for the democratization of the lingua franca:

> We need a lingua franca, and only one, if we are to be able to work out and implement efficient and fair solutions for our common problems on a European and on a global scale, and indeed if we are to be able to discuss, characterize and achieve linguistic justice itself. (LJ, p. 209)

Secondly, however, Réaume forcefully disputes that the existence of a lingua franca is 'a necessary precondition of robust democratic engagement and a vibrant transnational civil society'. She concedes that 'some movement across the linguistic divide must occur to have a conversation about matters of mutual interest', but argues that 'we should be able to ensure communication by encouraging multilingualism in a fairly small population', for example by 'promoting multiple language competence as an important qualification for employment in media organizations, the civil service, and the universities'. This suggestion reveals a frightening misperception of the nature and size of the task ahead, especially but not only in the context of the European Union, which is LJ's primary focus. What we need today, in Europe at any rate, is far more than press coverage and academic exchanges. What we need is the collective capacity to realize something tantamount to the construction of institutionalized solidarity at the level of nation states, and such a capacity has strong linguistic prerequisites.

Think, for example, of the linguistic challenge faced by the European Trade Union federation.[3] It is not just the huge cost and inconvenience of a large number of interpreting booths. To get the necessary level of trust, connivance and solidarity between German and Greek Trade Union leaders – not just between some aides specially recruited in view of their linguistic skills – you need them to be able to talk in *tête à tête*, make intelligible jokes and credible promises, using a language they both master sufficiently, just as the bosses of the employer organizations have been doing for quite a while. To have a good chance of Trade Union leaders sharing a common language at a sufficient level, knowledge of this language needs to be vigorously democratized throughout the European Union. Such democratization will not only produce leaders with the linguistic skills required for action in today's Europe but also activists able to mobilize cheaply across borders. Is this an illusory hope? Stephen May seems to think so. According to him (quoting Peter Ives), global English will never be able to fulfill the role of 'helping those marginalized and oppressed by "globalization" to be heard'. Having followed some of the bottom-up European Citizens initiatives which the Lisbon Treaty made possible, I can assure him that the linguistic hurdle can easily prove prohibitive, but at the same time that younger generations are in the process of overcoming it, thanks to their competence in English. How else could the marginalized, in Europe and beyond, manage to mobilize transnationally and be heard at the relevant level? Certainly not through the strategy Réaume deems sufficient. No doubt in the European Union as elsewhere the multilingualism of a handful of journalists, academics and civil servants could fulfill some needs, but definitely not those I am talking about and of which Réaume and May (excusably for non-Europeans) seem only very dimly aware.

Is the adoption of a lingua franca more damaging than it seems?

Réaume, however, has a third reason for objecting to my plea for the spreading of a lingua franca, namely that I underestimate the loss it imposes on those with another native language in terms of distributive justice. In order to address the inter-individual distributive injustice generated by the adoption a lingua franca, it is true that I advocate further disseminating the lingua franca. And in *LJ*, I recognize that, unlike what happens in a national context, the cost of this learning would remain borne by the respective linguistic communities rather than shared with the speakers of the dominant language. I argue, however, that the combination of subtitled broadcasting and films, exposure to the Internet, frequent contact with (mostly non-anglophone) foreigners and juvenile motivation will keep cheapening the effective dissemination of competence in English. Réaume doubts that substituting subtitling for dubbing can make a significant difference, though without providing evidence to counter the literature I refer to (*LJ*, § 3.7). More importantly, even if disseminating the lingua franca throughout the population could be done efficiently and cheaply, it would be pointless in terms of equality of opportunities, she says, for two reasons. Firstly, there are many other ways in which 'parents with means' will try to favor their offspring, including by 'purchasing better education in the lingua franca for their children, ensuring greater fluency and a better accent'. Secondly, the unequal access to English only matters for a small proportion of the population consisting of globetrotters.

To a twenty-first century European city dweller at any rate, this second reason sounds seriously out of touch: in most European countries, you certainly do not need to be a globetrotter to need English. Firstly, if you know English (and other languages), the Internet and the resources it offers enable you to trot the globe without leaving your chair. Secondly, the globe keeps trotting to you in the shape of visitors, clients and business partners who often speak far better English than your mother tongue. If this is the case, the second reason Réaume gives for challenging the relevance of English proficiency to opportunities does not stick, while the first reason becomes bizarre, indeed shocking: it sounds like arguing in a society in which many grow up illiterate that there is no point in their breaking the monopoly of the rich by learning to read and write since parents are bound to find other ways of favoring their children, including by purchasing a better education that will enable them to acquire a superior writing style.[4]

Before turning to Réaume's fourth and most fundament objection, let me briefly consider a variant of this third objection articulated by Stephen May. He also challenges my view that the spreading of the lingua franca will reduce inequalities. But he does so by pointing out that 'adoption of English as an official language of nation states has little influence on subsequent economic development'. There is, however, nothing in *LJ* that implies a correlation between the adoption of English or any other colonial language as its official language and a country's development. On the contrary, my 'ground floor' argument highlights the economic vulnerability of countries whose highly skilled citizens have acquired the lingua franca (*LJ*, § 5.10). Moreover, I point out the efficiency advantage of adopting as the official language the native language of the population (*LJ*, p. 157), a suggestion now confirmed by Laitin and Ramachandran's (2014) impressive empirical work. Yet, all of this is fully consistent with joining Amartya Sen (*LJ*, p. 238 fn 49), against Stephen May, in believing that democratizing competence in the lingua franca will help empower the vulnerable and break the monopoly that a 'small high-caste elite' would otherwise enjoy – which May seems to deny.

More serious than these disagreements, however, is May's apparent failure to understand my claim connecting the spreading of a lingua franca and the pursuit of social justice. He seems to understand it as asserting that the former serves the latter by 'enhancing social, economic and educational mobility in a globalized world'. My claim, spelled out and defended at length in chapter 1 of *LJ*, is rather that the pursuit of social justice requires strong institutions on a scale that reaches far beyond linguistically homogeneous communities and that the political feasibility and sustainability of such institutions has linguistic preconditions that can be satisfied only by the spreading of a lingua franca. My plea for the dissemination of the lingua franca as a way of reducing language-based inequalities of opportunities plays a more peripheral role regarding this connection: it indicates how best to alleviate the unavoidable impact on the linguistic dimension of inequality of opportunities that results from giving a privilege to the native language of part of the population concerned.

Let us now return to Denise Réaume and her fourth and most radical objection. Even if the measures I propose did provide effective ways of equalizing opportunities, they would still 'underscore how thin is the conception of equality animating the approach'. For what I propose in order to alleviate inter-individual injustice further contributes to the dominance of the lingua franca and thereby 'purchases an inadequate level of equal opportunity for individuals at the expense of inequality amongst language communities', more specifically by sacrificing 'the recognition of the equal status of all viable language communities participating in a joint political project'. As regards the EU's 24 official languages, this 'equality of status' matches quite neatly the official rhetoric of the European institutions. Réaume, however, believes that such multilingualism 'has never really been tried'. Chapter 4 of *LJ* is precisely devoted to a discussion of EU's cumbersome and expensive attempt to do exactly this, and to what I argue are its intrinsic limits. As Réaume rightly remarks, 'Europe is particularly challenging because of the number of official languages to be included and the further complication of the regional languages'. So is the world. But it is for Europe and the world, not for Canada or Belgium, that I am discussing how linguistic justice can best be pursued. And in such 'particularly challenging' contexts, equal status is a non-starter if it is meant to be more than a cosmetic strategy. So at least I argue at length in chapter 4, which Réaume does not discuss.

Is there an alternative? Yes there is. It consists in the territorial protection of weaker languages against the invasion of stronger ones, especially the lingua franca, as discussed in *LJ*'s longest chapter. Given Réaume's allergy to English dominance, I would have expected her to show more sympathy for this part of the book, but she dismisses this territorial strategy on the ground that it 'misunderstands the nature of the unfairness'. Her point is that if convergence on a lingua franca is neither inevitable nor beneficial,

> why should some have to settle for local status only while another community has both its home turf and the transnational arena as its linguistic terrain? We cannot solve the problem of unequal status in the transnational arena by giving each language group equal status in some *other* domain.

My response consists in a simple reasoning. One: a lingua franca is indispensable and urgent, as argued in *LJ*'s chapter 1. Two: the equal status strategy unavoidably bounces against narrow limits in a context with more than two or three languages, as argued in *LJ*'s chapter 4. Consequently, the territorial strategy developed in *LJ*'s chapter 5 offers the only serious approximation to what linguistic justice requires in this dimension of parity of esteem. Moreover, if it operates hand in hand with a successful democratization of the lingua franca, the distributive injustice in favor of anglophones which Réaume is so concerned about will not only be alleviated but reversed (*LJ*, § 3.9).

Does linguistic territoriality violate parity of esteem?

Whereas Denise Réaume's contribution offers the most developed argument against my plea for the dissemination of the lingua franca, Anna Stilz's contribution offers the most sustained argument against my plea for constraining this dissemination through the coercive protection of weaker languages. This plea is not based on the intrinsic value of linguistic diversity or on the right of languages to survive but on a conception of justice as parity of esteem.[5] In her challenge to this plea, which she summarizes correctly, Anna Stilz asks two questions.

Firstly, why is the systematic asymmetric bilingualism intrinsic to the promotion of a lingua franca necessarily an injustice in terms of parity of esteem, a failure of equal respect? Subjective identification with the weaker language is certainly a necessary condition for this to be the case. But, Stilz rightly argues, this cannot be a sufficient condition. We need a more demanding criterion 'to more successfully distinguish between reasonable and unreasonable complaints'. One possibility is that the asymmetry 'arises from a belief in the inferiority of my language, or of the people who speak it'. But, she points out, what drives the spreading of the lingua franca, according to my own analysis, is not such a belief but rather, as already mentioned the maximin dynamics. For an injustice to arise, she suggests instead, the asymmetry must derive from 'background power inequalities against which individual language-learning decisions take place', especially the global hegemony of the United States.

I am not sure that this condition identifies a proper subset of the situations of systematic asymmetric bilingualism. For I cannot imagine any such situation that would not derive, directly or indirectly, from power inequalities, often mainly via the lasting effect of these inequalities on the relative sizes of linguistic communities. Moreover, there are certainly situations in which the choice of the language of communication is clearly the reflection of past power relations – say when I communicate in English with locals in a Nigerian town – but in which no threat to parity of esteem is involved. As a specification of a sufficient condition for such a threat to arise, I would like to offer a different conjecture: in addition to people identifying with their weaker language, we need to be in a situation in which it is not unreasonable to expect that this weaker language should be known and used. This is what I was hinting at, though did not spell out, with my anecdote about the French journalist being denied a pint he had ordered in French in a Flemish bar (*LJ*, p. 118). Had he been believed to be a bona fide French tourist, his inability to speak Dutch would not have been perceived and sanctioned as a failure of equal respect. But the waiter believed him to be a Francophone Belgian citizen, and therefore interpreted his unwillingness or inability to speak Dutch as a violation of parity of esteem: as a member of a political community whose majority consists of Dutch speakers, a Francophone Belgian who does not speak Dutch when visiting Flanders raises the suspicion that he may not have bothered to learn Dutch out of contempt for a weaker language than his own. I believe this is the direction in which the answer to Anna Stilz's first question must be sought, and I suspect she would not disagree.

Stilz's second question concerns, not the identification of those cases in which injustice in terms of parity of esteem can be said to be present, but the way I propose to treat them. How can linguistic territoriality, that is a coercive regime that favors a local linguistic majority, possibly claim to satisfy parity of esteem? Does this not 'simply replicate the worrisome colonialist dynamic it was designed to prevent'? Would not an official multilingualism, possibly prorated as in Patten's (2014) variant, provide 'a superior approach to managing linguistic heterogeneity'? Of course, such a regime would not guarantee the survival of weaker languages, but what is at stake is 'a commitment to the equal dignity of *individuals*, not the equal dignity of *languages*'. And in order to prevent the formation of linguistic enclaves, such a regime of public support for minority languages is perfectly compatible, she argues, with the promotion of a common public language, which is not the same as linguistic homogeneity.

I do share the intuitions that underlie these claims, or at least I share them in the type of context which I expect Stilz to have in mind most spontaneously, what I shall call 'the US context': the domestic language is a very strong one, and the potential invaders are all weaker ones, where weakness and strength are defined in terms of relative (unconstrained) incentives to learn the other language (*LJ*, p. 140). Even in such a context, as Stilz and Patten both recognize, there may be room for legitimate constraints in order to increase the incentive and opportunity to learn more quickly the domestic language, but the justification of these constraints, when there is one, has nothing to do with parity of esteem. What may justify them is a concern for social cohesion, in a broad sense that encompasses economic opportunity, political participation and social interaction. In this 'US context', parity of esteem rather favors the maximal recognition and support for all minority languages, consistent with the domestic language being sufficiently often in maxi-min position for the virtuous circle leading to universal proficiency in that language to be permanently activated. I recognize this in *LJ*, when arguing that policies aimed at preserving or respecting local linguistic diversity 'can be a significant way of symbolically asserting the equal dignity of all languages and the associated identities' (*LJ*, p. 196).

The strong connection I assert between linguistic territoriality and parity of esteem simply does not exist in this 'US context'. But I claim that it does in what could be called 'the Québec context', where the potential invader is a stronger language. This stronger language is English in the Québec case, but can of course be other languages elsewhere – say, Spanish in Catalonia or French in Flanders – and the people carrying out the invasion need not only, nor even mainly, be native speakers of the invading language. In this context, the social cohesion argument in favor of territorial coercion is weaker, sometimes even worthless, as opportunity, participation and interaction could be promoted equally or even more efficiently by accelerating the acquisition of the stronger language. But this is, I claim, where the parity of esteem argument kicks in, along the three channels I discussed under the headings 'colonial attitudes', 'kindness-driven agony' and 'every tongue a queen'.

Under Stilz's or Patten's preferred accommodating regime of pro-rated multilingualism, the maxi-min dynamics will perpetuate the asymmetric 'bowing'. This would be unjust in terms of parity of esteem, not because the invading language owes its strength to 'background power inequalities', but because – and to the extent that – it would not be unreasonable to expect the natives (and other speakers) of the stronger language to learn and use the weaker local language. The courage and humility to learn and use a weaker language cannot be reasonably expected from tourists or participants in international meetings, but it can from people who intend to become permanent residents of the territory concerned. Is this not overkill, at the expense of the equal dignity of local linguistic minorities? It is not if, as in the pursuit of social cohesion, no more coercive measures are taken as regards public education and public communication than those required to drive the local language sufficiently into maxi-min position, consistently with respect for freedom in the private use of languages. And it must, moreover, be consistent with a principle of reciprocity, however, counterfactual (*LJ*, § 5.6).

This discussion of Stilz's stimulating challenges also provides an answer to Daniel Weinstock's claim that my parity of esteem argument in favor of linguistic territoriality holds only in 'colonial cases'. It holds, he argues, when the pressure to learn and use the stronger language is driven by colonial attitudes nourished by an unjust background of oppression, but not in the 'mere number cases', where the maxi-min dynamics suffices to propagate the stronger language. The fact that I welcome this mechanism as a powerful instrument for the democratization of the lingua franca does not bar me from asserting that it can lead to an injustice even if it is the only mechanism at work. And I claim that there is an injustice in terms of parity of esteem if a linguistic community is not allowed to take measures (consistent with fundamental liberties) in order to counteract the unfair 'asymmetric bowing' spontaneously induced by linguistic inequality in situations in which it is not unreasonable to expect symmetry. This is what a territorial linguistic regime aims to achieve. Even in the absence of background political or economic oppression, the persistent refusal of speakers of stronger languages to make the effort of learning and using the language of the community among which they have chosen to settle could rightly be regarded as a deviation from justice as parity of esteem.

What emerges from this discussion, more clearly I hope than in *LJ* but consistently with it, is that my concern for justice as parity of esteem leads to the defense of something like Patten's (2014, 225) 'hybrid thesis', that is a position that leaves space for the equal (pro tanto) recognition of all native languages present in a territory while asserting the legitimacy of constraints favoring the locally dominant language.[6] What the right balance is between these two elements will vary from one situation to another: as one moves from the 'US case' to the 'Québec case' and beyond, as the invading language gets stronger relative to the local one, the justification for linguistic constraints on public communication and education gains strength. And my key point, admittedly counterintuitive for native speakers of powerful languages in their home environment, is that it is not only on grounds of social cohesion but also of parity of esteem, that equal recognition must be denied.

Does the justification of linguistic territoriality need to appeal to parity of esteem?

Along with Anna Stilz, Jean Laponce, Rainer Bauböck and Daniel Weinstock, all doubt that parity of esteem can favor a coercive territorial regime over an accommodating regime. Nonetheless, unlike Stilz, all three believe that linguistic territoriality can be justified on a different basis. Jean Laponce's justification rests on 'the premise that nations have the right to govern themselves either independently or, if they prefer, autonomously within a larger polity'. This right is meant not as a legally enforceable right, but as a moral right subject to restrictions of viability and respect of individual rights. In *LJ*, I briefly consider what Laponce calls 'the fundamental human right of nations to self determination' as a possible justification of linguistic territoriality, and dismiss it on the ground that it is incompatible with the adoption of global justice as the ultimate standard:

> Nations, politically organized peoples [...] are sheer instruments to be created and dismantled, structured and absorbed, empowered and constrained, in the service of justice in a sense that far from reduces to fundamental liberties. Consequently, whether a territorial linguistic regime is legitimate is not a question that can be settled by appealing to national sovereignty, but rather one that needs to be settled in order to determine how extensive national sovereignty is allowed to be. (*LJ*, p. 139)

In other words, the language of fundamental rights of nations seems to be inadequate to characterize a just world. And the relevant question, when assessing secession or greater autonomy, immigration or linguistic policy, is therefore not what a nation has the right to do but whether what is being proposed that it should do makes (or is likely to trigger a process that will make) the world less unjust than it currently is. What makes a linguistic regime just is therefore not a question that can be settled by national self-determination, but rather one that needs to be answered in order to determine the just limits to whatever may be called national self-determination.

Rainer Bauböck, by contrast, appeals to the universal right of *individuals* to participate in a self-governing community – not to the fundamental right of nations to govern themselves – and therefore escapes the dismissal articulated in *LJ* (§ 5.2). In order to be self-governing, Bauböck argues, a community needs to have control over a territory, and its members must share a language, both to make communication possible between them and to demarcate the community from the outside. Let us agree that there is a universal right to political participation and leave aside the question of whether such a right matters in itself or only as an instrument for the effective pursuit of justice (see Van Parijs 2011b, chapter 1). A common medium of communication is certainly a major factor for the good functioning of a self-governing community. But why could the common medium not become English in Québec or Spanish in Catalonia? I can see that having a distinct language can strengthen national identity, and nation builders have been making generous use of this potential, but the adoption of an official language that serves to demarcate one's self-governing community from the outside world is certainly no necessary condition for securing the right to participate in a self-governing community, as illustrated, for example, by the number of countries that adopted Spanish or English as their official language. When a stronger language could plausibly serve the function of a public language just as well as the weaker local language, we need a different argument for defending the territorial protection of this weaker language as a matter of justice. And this ground, I argue, can be provided by justice as parity of esteem, once we understand that equal recognition does not secure the latter in a context of potential invasion by a stronger language. Nonetheless, I believe Bauböck is right to draw attention to the existence of a strong connection between linguistic territoriality and self-government, but the derivation runs in the other direction: it is not self-government that calls for linguistic territoriality, but linguistic territoriality that calls for self-government. Once a population is given and exercises the right to protect its language within a territory, a particularly strong version of the subsidiarity principle kicks in to support a high degree of autonomy for that territory, so that the people can govern themselves in the language most familiar to them.

In a similar vein, Daniel Weinstock claims that linguistic territoriality can be justified – in those situations where he thinks it can – only 'on the basis of the value of democracy and self-determination':

> In the same way that it can decide to invest more or less in its public transport system, or in its public libraries, or in its parks, on the basis of the results of democratic deliberation and democratic processes, a group can decide to enact legislation aimed at protecting its vulnerable language against the predictable impact of interaction with other, stronger languages.

This protective legislation has a cost – most significantly in the form of dissuasion of potentially useful immigrants – and some linguistic communities may not care sufficiently about their ancestral language to be willing to pay that cost. 'A liberal democratic ethics will however require that [a group] make use of coercion as parsimoniously as possible, and that it recognize that certain violations of individual rights cannot be undertaken, no matter what the consequences'.

I disagree with none of this (see *LJ*, pp. 169–171). Nonetheless, I claim that a grounding in justice is needed for the implementation of the territorial protection of a language which is not needed for the collective decision to produce other public goods. Democratically organized communities can decide, but they must be guided by considerations of justice. And it is therefore important to know whether justice is also to be conceived as parity of esteem and, if so, whether it recommends an accommodating or a coercive regime. What I am assuming here is that there is a set of issues that are neither settled by a list of fundamental rights which the international community might see as its job to impose on democratic majorities nor left completely up for each political community to decide on according to its collective evaluations of the costs and benefits of public goods. If justice required an accommodating linguistic regime (just as it recommends, in my opinion too, an accommodating religious regime), the public good of language maintenance could still be pursued through subsidies if the community finds this a good use for its tax money, but not through the coercive imposition of the language of public communication and public education which defines linguistic territoriality. In a framework like mine which gives priority to justice and sees 'the value of democracy and self determination' as instrumental rather than fundamental, appealing to the latter can never be sufficient to justify a coercive regime.

Is linguistic territoriality too feeble?

Whether justified or not, Weinstock also doubts that a territorial regime that respects fundamental liberties 'will succeed in arresting the sociolinguistic processes that lead to the spread of English as a *lingua franca* just at the point at which it comes to threaten bilingualism'. According to him, 'the main reason is that though moderate policies can increase the level of competence in the weaker language on a territory, they cannot increase the level of *use* of that language'. The latter statement is not correct. An acceptable territorial regime cannot govern directly the private use of language, but the exclusive use of the official language in public communication will directly affect the use of languages in administrative procedures. More significantly, by imposing the language in which the young are educated and by providing adults with incentives to learn it, public policies multiply the number of situations in which the official language will turn out to be the maxi-min language. It will therefore tend to be spontaneously used, instead of the international lingua franca, among people who do not have the same native tongue. It will also tend to be used, especially on some subjects and from the second generation, among immigrants with the same native language. The direct and above all indirect impact of a liberally acceptable language regime on language use – and thereby in turn on the opportunity and motivation to maintain and improve the knowledge of the official language – can therefore be considerable.

Nonetheless, I agree with Weinstock that there is no guarantee that the strongest coercive regime consistent with fundamental liberties and a cost deemed worth paying by a democratic majority of the population will suffice to support universal competence in a weaker local language. This is certainly true in a context characterized by high levels of migration, easy access to foreign media worldwide and universal spreading of a common lingua franca at ever higher levels of proficiency. In *LJ*, I argue that there is something sad but in principle nothing wrong with 'fair resignation', at least if the background were one of just worldwide distribution of resources (*LJ*, §5.14). Stephen May rightly points out that 'subject to the unregulated vicissitudes of the maxi-min principle, [the poorest and/or least powerful] would have likely lost their languages long before any coercive territorial regime could come charging to the rescue'. In my book I recognize this explicitly (*LJ*, p. 174), but I also claim that nothing serious can be done about it, besides trying to create the conditions, including linguistic, for the pursuit of worldwide distributive justice. As Denise Réaume neatly puts it, 'the important questions of language policy start not with what is feasible, but with what is just'. And a smart struggle for greater justice will help make feasible tomorrow what is not feasible today.

Disclosure statement
No potential conflict of interest was reported by the author.

Notes
1. Along the same line, see *LJ*, p. 34 ('Global English or, as it is now sometimes called, Globish is a dialect of English whose spoken form in particular is more difficult to master for some of those who grew up hearing nothing but Oxford or Dallas English than for many native speakers of Italian or Bengali'.) and the illustrative anecdotes in footnote 48.
2. Denise Réaume correctly interprets the use I make of the maxi-min dynamics as purely descriptive and explanatory, not normative. Nowhere in LJ is there an 'advocacy of the maxi-min principle' (curiously attributed to me by Stephen May), only a conjecture about the central mechanism of language spreading under contemporary conditions.
3. As vividly explained by Bernadette Ségol, secretary general of the European Trade Union Confederation in the discussion that followed a lecture she gave at Université St Louis, Brussels on 15 October 2013.
4. While agreeing with me that competence in English as a common lingua franca needs to be accelerated, Jean Laponce claims that 'the spread of a needed lingua

franca is not a factor equalizing social conditions. It is more likely to sustain and possibly increase social cleavages'. The analogy with literacy should suffice to undermine the plausibility of this claim.

5. Consequently, I confess I have great difficulty understanding Stephen May's ascribing to me a 'reductionist account of language, by which language is viewed in terms of its communicative uses and reach and not in relation to its symbolic and identity functions'. May did notice, however, that I 'concede' that 'languages come to be formally (and informally) associated with particular ethnic and national identities'. I do indeed, to the point of devoting one-third of the book to the implications of this 'concession'.

6. See, in the same direction, my response to the comments by Jan Velaers and Helder De Schutter in Van Parijs (2011c), especially §§ 6 and 8.

Notes on contributor

Philippe Van Parijs is a professor at the University of Louvain, where he has directed the Hoover Chair of Economic and Social Ethics since its creation in 1991. He is also a Special Guest Professor at the University of Leuven and a Senior Research Fellow at Nuffield College, Oxford. He is one of the founders of the Basic Income Earth Network and chairs its International Board. His books include *Evolutionary Explanation in the Social Sciences* (1981), *Le Modèle économique et ses rivaux* (1990), *Qu'est-ce qu'une société juste?* (1991), *Marxism Recycled* (1993), *Real Freedom for All* (1995), *Éthique économique et sociale* (2000, with C. Arnsperger), *What's Wrong with a Free Lunch?* (2001), *L'Allocation universelle* (2005, with Y. Vanderborght), *Just Democracy. The Rawls-Machiavelli Program* (2011) and *Linguistic Justice for Europe and for the World* (2011, paperback 2015).

References

De Schutter, H., 2014. Intralinguistic justice. Unpublished paper discussed at the Fung Global Fellows Seminar at Princeton University on December 12th, 2013.

Laitin, D. and Ramachandran, R., 2014. *Language policy and economic development*. Palo Alto: Stanford University, Department of Political Science.

Patten, A., 2014. *Equal recognition. The moral foundations of minority rights*. Princeton: Princeton University Press.

Van Parijs, P., 2011a. *Linguistic justice for Europe and for the world*. Oxford: Oxford University Press. Paperback 2015. German edition: *Sprachengerechtigkeit für Europa und die Welt*. Frankfurt: Suhrkamp, 2013. Dutch edition: *Taal en rechtvaardigheid voor Europa en de wereld*. Tielt: Lannoo, 2015.

Van Parijs, P., 2011b. *Just democracy. The Rawls-Machiavelli programme*. Colchester: ECPR Press.

Van Parijs Philippe, 2011c. On linguistic territoriality and Belgium's linguistic future. A reply. *In*: *The linguistic territoriality principle. Right violation or parity of esteem?*, 53–77. Brussels: Re-Bel e-book n°11. Available from: www.rethinkingbelgium.eu. Reprinted in P. Popelier et al., eds. 2012. Belgium: *Quo Vadis?*, 35–60 Antwerp: Intersentia.

Index

INDEX

INDEX

INDEX

INDEX